A Collection of Afghans

Trexler Designs

Edited by Carolyn Sheffield

Andrews and McMeel
A Universal Press Syndicate Company
Kansas City • New York

Acknowledgments

The following yarn companies and designers are responsible for the beautiful afghan patterns found in this book. Thanks to each and every one for their cooperation and talents:

Brunswick Yarn   Margaret Brainard
Bucilla   Peggy McConnell
Caron Yarns   Stephanie Roselle
Coats & Clark   Mary Ann Sipes
Unger Yarn

A Collection of Afghans copyright © 1989 by Universal Press Syndicate. All rights reserved. Printed in the United States. No part of this book may be used or reproduced in any manner without written permission except in the case of reprints in the context of reviews. For information write Andrews and McMeel, a Universal Press Syndicate Company, 4900 Main Street, Kansas City, Missouri 64112.

Library of Congress Cataloging-in-Publication Data

A Collection of afghans / by Trexler Designs.
   p. cm.
  ISBN 0–8362–1860–4 : $8.95
  1. Afghans (Coverlets) 2. Crocheting—
Patterns.
  3. Knitting—Patterns. I. Trexler Designs.
  TT825.C645 1989
  746.9'7041—dc20   89–36293
                        CIP

Cover: A cardinal in winter—always welcome both inside and out! The cardinal in the evergreens is worked into this cheerful afghan as you crochet. No need to add any embroidery. Directions on page 27. Yarn for the cover afghan courtesy of Brunswick Yarns.

Attention: Schools and Businesses

Andrews and McMeel books are available at quantity discounts with bulk purchase for educational, business, or sales promotional use. For information, please write to: Special Sales Department, Andrews and McMeel, 4900 Main Street, Kansas City, Missouri 64112.

Contents

Introduction, 4

Afghans, 5

Needles, Hooks, Etc., 8

Yarn, 9

Gauge, 10

Terms, Abbreviations and Symbols, 10

Knitting, 12

Crocheting, 18

Finishing, 23

Conversion Charts, 26

Instructions, 26

Cardinal Afghan, 27

Monk's Cloth Afghan, 30

Photographs, 33–48

Aran Crochet, 49

Aran Knit, 51

Fisherman, 55

Pretty Petals, 56

Lullaby Baby Afghan, 58

Indian Blanket, 59

Traditional Ripple, 61

Quick Popcorn, 62

Quick and Easy Diamonds, 63

Delightful Pennsylvania Dutch, 64

Plaid, 65

Honeycomb, 66

Mad for Plaid, 68

X-Cellent Choice for a Sailor, 69

Tropical Flowers Afghan & Pillow, 73

Shamrock Afghan, 77

Outstanding Knit Irish Lace, 79

Introduction

Soon after I started writing my syndicated column, "Pat's Pointers," twenty-five years ago, I learned from my readers that afghans are very precious to people. An afghan is a family treasure to be cherished as an heirloom and used by generation after generation.

Knowing how popular afghans are, we decided to compile this collection of our favorite afghan patterns—some old and some new. The following pages present a broad scope of patterns. Whether you choose to knit, crochet or weave an afghan, there is one for you. Classic, plaid, embroidered and Aran fisherman designs are all here. Eager beginners and seasoned pros alike will find an afghan to warm the heart and the home.

But that's not all. In addition to these distinctive patterns, we have included a how-to section and a reference guide. Select your project, begin one of the most enjoyable, rewarding needlecraft experiences—a lovely handmade afghan—and enjoy!

—PAT TREXLER

Afghans

As you work on an afghan, have you ever wondered about the word "afghan"? Does it really come from Afghanistan? And if so, why? What about the early knitters and crocheters? Where did the crafts start? How did they evolve?

An afghan, according to Webster, is a blanket or a shawl of colored wool, knit or crocheted in strips or squares that are joined together by sewing or crocheting. It is also a Turkoman carpet woven in geometric designs. Apparently, our brightly colored afghan patterns and designs are similar to the rugs and blankets of Afghanistan; hence, the name afghan, first used in the 1830s.

In the history of knitting and crocheting, there is little mention of afghans. When they are mentioned, it is usually in relation to wars. In times of war, patriotic women and even children knit and crocheted afghans and other items for the soldiers. Knit and crocheted items were also sold to raise money to help the war effort.

More information is available on knitting and crocheting, the crafts primarily used to make afghans. Knit, an old word, originally meant to fuse (as in broken bones), to draw together (as in knitting brows), to join, to marry, and to tie or knot. Knitting is defined today as making a fabric by intertwining yarn or thread in a series of connected loops. Knitting uses needles to form and pull the loops through the existing loops.

Although knitting is thought to be more than 2,000 years old by some, others believe that the earliest fabrics were woven, or worked in other techniques that look similar to knitting. Some believe shepherds in ancient times may have been the first knitters.

Many sources think knitting started in Arabia. It is believed that the Arab traders knit on frames while they rode their camel caravans to Egypt and India. Knit pieces have been found in Egyptian tombs dating back to A.D. 400, but there is controversy over the method used to make the fabric.

Crochet, thought by most to be a newer craft, is named for the French word "croche," meaning little hook. Crochet now means to make needlework by looping thread with a hooked needle. Crochet probably started as finger crochet, pulling a loop through a loop.

Like most old crafts, the origins of crochet are not easy to discover. One source tells us that crochet hooks have been traced back to the time of Christ. Others think the craft developed in 16th-century Europe, possibly in Italy, later spreading to Spain, France and Ireland. Other sources think crocheting developed in Scotland among the shepherds watching their flocks. Although the origin is somewhat obscure, most sources believe crochet was developed comparatively late.

Between the 13th and 16th centuries, lacemaking was nun's work. French nuns, thought to be the first to use a hook for lace, would take laces apart to determine how they were made. Then, they would adapt the pattern for crochet, which was much faster to work than needle or bobbin laces. French nuns brought crocheted lace to Ireland in an exhibit in Dublin in 1772.

By the 16th century, knitting guilds flourished throughout Europe. During a six-year apprenticeship, the apprentice spent three years serving and learning in his master's shop. The next three years were spent in foreign travel to study other methods and designs. To become a master knitter, the apprentice knit a pair of stockings, a woolen waistcoat (shirt), a cap and a carpet of his own design, all in thirteen weeks. If the masters of the guild approved, he then became a master knitter. Some guilds continued into the 18th century.

In the late 1500s, William Lee, an Englishman, upset over the amount of time his fiancee spent knitting, became the first to take a scientific approach to knitting. He invented a machine to knit stockings, which although still slow, was faster than hand knitting. At this time, hand knitting was an established part of society and a source of income for many. Thinking the machine would damage the hand knitting industry, Queen Elizabeth I refused to give Mr. Lee a patent.

Two-color knitting, known as Fair Isle, is very popular in Norway and the Shetland Islands. There is no way of knowing who developed the technique first. Both use many of the same features and techniques. Sometimes more than a dozen colors are used although only two colors are used in any one row.

There is also the possibility of influence from the Spaniards. In 1588, as the Spanish Armada was escaping through the Norwegian Sea, many ships were lost in the rough seas, or washed onto the Shetland Islands. Fair Isle designs may have had their beginnings in the sweaters worn by the sailors who were washed ashore. It is strange, though, that nothing was known of Fair Isle knitting until Fair Isle caps were mentioned over 200 years later in 1822 in a book by Samuel Hibbert about the Shetland Islands.

In Colonial America, girls learned at an early age to knit. Believers in the Puritan morality felt that busy hands pleased the Lord and kept the devil from influencing their thoughts. Many four-year-olds could knit stockings and mittens. They began with heavy yarn and progressed to finer ones. After our independence from England, more supplies were available and techniques were refined. Schools taught the children more sophisticated needlework. Spinning, weaving and knitting parties were social events as well as productive.

In the 1800s, crocheting finally became popular. During the Potato Famine in Ireland, nuns taught thousands of women and children to crochet. The lace was then sold to buy food. Needlework became part of the educational system, being taught to the students and also used as a source of income to support the schools. When Queen Victoria received table linens with crochet edges, crochet became the rage for high society. A crocheted gown became the only appropriate dress for christening a child. Suitors, hoping to win the hearts of young women, would bring crocheted gifts. After the famine, crocheting became a leisure time activity.

As early as the 1830s, knitting and crocheting patterns were being published in *Godey's Lady's Book*. In 1854, Mrs. Ann S. Stephens, in *The Ladies Complete Guide to Crochet, Fancy Knitting and Needlework*, described crochet as "one of those gentle means by which women are kept feminine and ladylike in this fast age." In 1899, John Paton Son & Company became the first yarn company to publish its own patterns to promote its yarns, now a common practice.

In the 1840s, crocheting came to America, brought by the Irish fleeing the famine. Instead of continuing to imitate old laces, the Americans started working new patterns and adapting patterns from patchwork quilts. Pinwheels, spider webs and cross stitch patterns worked in filet crochet became popular. Simple loops of chain, popcorn stitches as well as old patterns such as stars and pineapple designs were used.

During wartime, women have always supported the soldiers by knitting warm socks, hats, gloves, scarves and afghans. In addition to sending these to the soldiers, the women would also sell their knit goods to provide money for the soldiers' aid groups.

Anne Macdonald, in her book *No Idle Hands* tells about an article in a daily paper printed during the Civil War. The article directed people to these sales with this advice: "What is called an 'afghan' would to the uninstructed mind, appear, perhaps as absurd an article as ever was devised for the use of man. Not so, however, to the few persons of enlightened intelligence. Few things ... are more essential to a gentleman; in fact life is a burden without one."

During World War I, even Girl Scout troops were making knit articles for the soldiers, sometimes including notes to tell which Girl Scout troop made the items. Many troops made afghans to support the war.

Mrs. Calvin Coolidge entered a knitting contest in 1923. The judges, unaware of who had submitted the entries, awarded an honorable mention to Mrs. Coolidge for a baby afghan called "Slumberland Afghan." Many people offered to buy it, but Mrs. Coolidge kept the afghan for her first grandchild. Mrs. Coolidge also knit a bedspread, which was featured in a knitting booklet. A replica of that spread is now in the Smithsonian Institution in Washington.

Aran knitting, named for the Aran Isles off the west coast of Ireland and also known as fisherman knitting, has many romantic legends. It was thought that different patterns were almost like a coat of arms for a family. Many meanings have been given to the many intricate patterns, which are said to date back hundreds of years. Supposedly, if a sailor was lost at sea, his family could identify him by his Aran sweater.

Evidence, not nearly as fascinating, indicates Aran knitting may be a product of the 20th century. Prior to this century, there had never been any indication of Aran knitting in the arts, photography or literature of the islands. In writings about the sweaters of these areas, bobbles and the very intricate designs were never mentioned. According to a museum in Dublin, there is reason to think that Aran knitting was brought to the Aran Isles from America. An Irish immigrant to the United States was taught the craft in New England. Cables were already common on the British ganseys (traditional British pullovers). When the immigrant returned to Ireland, the new skills were incorporated into the basic design of the common gansey.

By the late 19th century, crocheting was emerging as a well-established craft. There were, by that time, many publications with crochet instructions. In the 1920s, the yarn companies were sponsoring contests with cash prizes to foster the popularity of crochet. These contests continued into the 1940s. Speed contests to determine who could crochet the longest edge in one hour were covered on the radio by well-known celebrities.

Soon crocheting was no longer confined to only laces and edgings, although they still remained popular. People began to use yarns other than the fine crochet cottons to make larger items. Soft fabrics were used for rugs.

Crocheting is now used for sweaters, rugs, place mats, baby clothes, scarves, mittens, hats, purses—and, of course, afghans!

During World War II, women continued to make afghans as well as other knit items. Many were made with assorted colored squares. Afghans of colored squares were also made during the Korean War to send to the homeless in Korea. It is estimated that 14,000 children's sweaters and afghans were sent to Korea. To save time, sometimes the squares were sent unassembled along with some yarn so the children could sew them together.

In peaceful times, people everywhere enjoy afghans for the warmth and homey look they provide. They are used as decorative accessories as well as being functional. Afghans conjure up thoughts of fireplaces, good books and relaxation. What could be nicer than cuddling under a soft, cozy afghan, perhaps watching television, as you knit or crochet another beautiful afghan?

Needles, Hooks, Etc.

Knitting Needles: Almost everyone, even non-knitters, is familiar with straight knitting needles, available in 10- and 14-inch lengths, usually made of aluminum, plastic or sometimes wood. Ordinary needle sizes range from 0 to 15, the larger the number, the larger the needle size. For several strands of yarn or bulky yarns, larger needles are also available in sizes 17, 19, 35 and 50.

Circular needles are double pointed and connected by a thin, flexible nylon piece. They are used for knitting back and forth or in the round. Circular needles are available in lengths ranging from 11 to 36 inches. Jumper needles come in pairs, usually in 20-inch lengths. They are similar to circular needles but have only one point connected to a thin, flexible nylon piece, ending with a stopper.

Circular and jumper needles, developed in Norway in the 1920s, can be used anytime a straight needle is used. Because circular and jumper needles are longer than straight needles, they are capable of holding more stitches and distributing the weight more evenly. This is an important plus for older or arthritic knitters, although many young people also prefer circular needles. In crowded places, you'll find the ends of the needles will not get in the way. When you put your work down, just push it onto the thin section of the needle to prevent stretching and ridges. You'll also find you seldom lose a circular needle because it is all one piece.

Of course, there are some disadvantages to circular needles. When they come from the package, they are usually curly. Just using them will control some of the curls. If they are too difficult, place them in very hot water to remove the kinks. Often the sizes are not marked on circular needles. A needle gauge, normally found on a stitch gauge, will be needed to determine your needle size.

Most knitters feel strongly about straight needles vs. circular needles. Try both and decide for yourself!

Crochet hooks: Crochet hooks are available in steel, aluminum, plastic and sometimes wood.

Aluminum and plastic hooks, the most commonly used hooks, may have a size expressed in numbers, letters or both. Sizes range from B/1 to K/10½, with B/1 the smallest and K/10½ the largest of the regular hooks. L, M, N, P, Q and S hooks are also available for bulky yarns or working several strands together. See chart on page 26.

Wood hooks, although not as widely available, come in longer lengths and larger sizes. Afghan hooks, with one end like a crochet hook and the other like a knitting needle (the opposite end from the point), are usually in 10- and 14-inch lengths. Afghan hooks are used for afghan stitch.

Etc: Other tools are sometimes used to make your knitting or crocheting easier. Of course, you will need scissors and a ruler. A crochet hook is usually needed by knitters for picking up dropped stitches or working an edging. A yarn needle with a large eye and a blunt point is useful for sewing motifs or panels together.

A stitch gauge is a useful accessory. Most have a 2-inch opening to check your gauge (very important!), a 5- or 6-inch ruler and holes to check your needle or hook size.

If your pattern has cables, you will need a cable needle (also called a cable hook or cable stitch holder), available in several shapes and sizes. If your afghan has a multicolored pattern, you may need yarn bobbins, usually a flat plastic piece that holds a small amount of yarn and eliminates some of the tangles of changing colors.

Stitch markers are also available and very helpful when working several patterns in one afghan. Stitch markers placed between the patterns make the knitting much easier. Think of a stitch marker as a guide telling you when the pattern changes, thus eliminating a lot of counting.

Yarn

Most afghan patterns are worked in worsted-weight yarn, still the best-known and most widely used yarn. Sport-weight yarn can also be used for a finer, lighter afghan. Each pattern will recommend the weight yarn that should be used for that afghan.

Both worsted-weight and sport-weight yarns are available in many fibers, including natural animal fibers, natural plant fibers and man-made fibers. Natural fibers, often used for garments, are seldom used for afghans. Wool, the most popular animal fiber, refers primarily to the fleece from sheep, but also applies to alpaca, mohair, cashmere and other animal fleece. Alpaca, from a South American relative of the llama, is long, silky and fairly lightweight. Mohair, with its soft, lightweight and warm, fluffy appearance, is very popular. Cashmere, the prestigious yarn from the Kashmir goat of the Himalayas, is a fine, soft, lightweight and expensive yarn. Nothing can match the natural resiliency, warmth and durability of wool along with its wonderful, soft touch. However, some people are allergic to wools and need to consider other yarns. Dry cleaning is recommended for wool.

Man-made fibers include polyester, acrylic, orlon and other synthetic fibers. Synthetics are usually warm, resilient, easy-care, inexpensive yarns, and therefore very popular. These soft, durable yarns are available in a wide variety of colors. Blends, often with the advantages of each fiber used, are also widely available. Your choice is determined only by your personal preference.

Most yarns have a dye lot number on the label. Yarns dyed at different times can vary in shade. They may not look noticeably different, but the difference can often be seen in the completed afghan or garment. Be sure to buy enough yarn in the same dye lot. It is wise to buy more than the pattern recommends. Reputable yarn stores will usually allow you to return unopened skeins of yarn within a reasonable length of time.

Many people mistakenly believe that "ply" determines the weight or circumference of the yarn. Ply refers only to the number of strands twisted together to form the finished yarn. Four-ply means four strands of yarn are twisted together; three-ply means three strands are twisted together. If three very fine strands are twisted together, obviously this yarn would be thinner than another three-ply with three thick strands of yarn. Therefore, do not rely on ply. Concentrate on the gauge and the weight of the yarn.

Gauge

It's surprising how many people never check their gauge. If you make a sweater or any garment, the gauge is the most important indication of the fit. Always work a sample swatch before beginning any project. Gauge is not as important with an afghan because the afghan doesn't need to fit; however, if your gauge is off, the afghan could come out much smaller or larger than you had planned. The amount of yarn needed to complete the afghan may also be affected.

Besides checking your gauge, working a sample swatch will also help you become familiar with the pattern stitch. Cast on enough stitches to equal 4 inches. For example, if the gauge is 5 stitches per inch, cast on 20 stitches. Work in the pattern stitch for 4 inches. You should now have a swatch exactly 4 inches square. If it is wider than 4 inches, try a smaller needle. If it is less than 4 inches wide, change to a larger needle. Count your rows if a row gauge is given; however, if the stitch gauge is correct, do not change needles to adjust the row gauge.

Let's say your afghan has a gauge of 5 stitches to the inch and you have cast on 250 stitches. Your finished afghan will measure 50 inches wide (250 stitches divided by 5 stitches per inch equals 50 inches).

If your swatch shows a gauge of $4\frac{1}{2}$ stitches to the inch instead of the recommended 5 stitches, your afghan will be $55\frac{1}{2}$ inches wide. You need to use a smaller needle to get the correct gauge.

If your gauge is $5\frac{1}{2}$ stitches to the inch, your afghan will be a little more than 45 inches. You need to try a larger needle.

Check your gauge occasionally on the afghan, too. When you do this, count the stitches and rows over a 2-inch span. Don't ignore half stitches. Even quarter stitches will affect the finished size.

Terms, Abbreviations and Symbols

To a beginner, knit and crochet patterns often look like a foreign language. Don't be intimidated by what at first seems gibberish. It actually is a shorthand that helps the needleworker. You will soon see that the terms, abbreviations and symbols eliminate repetitious instructions and make lengthy directions much shorter and concise. This in turn speeds up understanding.

Terms: The terms for both knit and crochet are included. Each definition will indicate if it is a knit or crochet term. Terms are in alphabetical order.

Bar: the upright or vertical part of a crochet stitch.

Bind off: to fasten off knit stitches in a secure way.

Block: either 1) square motif; or 2) shaping an afghan or garment, usually with the aid of steam or water.

Bobbin: device, usually plastic, to hold small amounts of yarn when working with several colors.

Break off: to cut yarn.

Cast on: method of putting the first row of stitches onto the knitting needle.

End right side: complete row on front (right) side.

End wrong side: complete row on back (wrong) side.

Fasten off: cut yarn 4 to 6 inches from work, slip through loop on needle or hook, pull tight to knot. Weave end into wrong side of work.

Garter stitch: knit each row.

Mark row or stitch: place a marker or pin, or loosely tie a contrasting piece of yarn, in place indicated.

Multiple: number of stitches needed to complete one pattern design. A multiple of 4 would be 4, 8, 12 or any number divisible by 4. If a pattern calls for a multiple of 4 stitches plus 2, just add 2 to the multiple of 4; for example, 6, 10, 14, 18 and so on.

Post: upright or vertical part of a crochet stitch; same as bar.

Right side: front, or side shown to the public.

Round: work done in one direction with right side always facing you.

Row: horizontal line of work. Work is turned to work the next row.

Stockinette stitch: knit 1 row, purl 1 row. The knit side (flat) is the right side. The purl side (bumpy) is the wrong side.

Turn: turn the work so the reverse side faces you. Usually done at the end of a row.

Turning chain: chain stitches worked at the end of a crochet row. The turning chain often counts as the first stitch of the next row.

Work even: work pattern as established without increases or decreases.

Wrong side: reverse of right side; side normally not seen.

Abbreviations are used for all forms of a word including both singular and plural except where indicated. For example, dec means decrease, decreases, decreased and decreasing.

Any abbreviations other than those listed here that are used in a pattern will be included in the directions. Abbreviations are in alphabetical order.

Crochet only:

ch	chain
dc	double crochet
dtr	double treble crochet
hdc	half double crochet
sc	single crochet
tr	treble crochet
tr tr	triple treble crochet

Knit only:

cn	cable needle
k	knit
p	purl
psso	pass slip stitch over
St st	stockinette stitch

Knit and crochet:

beg	begin(ning)	sk	skip
CC	contrasting color	sl	slip
dec	decrease	sl st	slip stitch
inc	increase	sp(s)	space(s)
lp(s)	loop(s)	st(s)	stitch(es)
MC	main color	tog	together
p	picot	yo	yarn over
rnd(s)	round(s)		

Symbols: The same symbols are used in both knit and crochet.

Asterisks (*) are used to indicate the beginning of a sequence that will be repeated. For example, "*dc in 2nd st, ch 1, repeat from * 2 more times," means "dc in 2nd st, ch 1, dc in 2nd st, ch 1, dc in 2nd st, ch 1." Work the original directions following the asterisk, then repeat them as many times as directed. Sometimes directions will tell you to work the instructions between the asterisks. If another repeat is in the pattern, the pattern may use double asterisks (**) to differentiate from the single asterisk (*).

Parentheses ( ) indicate that instructions within the parentheses are to be repeated. For example, "(sc, dc) 2 times" means "sc, dc, sc, dc."

Brackets [ ] are used only inside parentheses. For example, "(k2, [k2tog] 2 times, p2) twice" means "k2, k2tog, k2tog, p2, k2, k2tog, k2tog, p2."

Knitting

There are only two basic stitches in knitting, the knit stitch and the purl stitch. Once you've mastered knitting and purling, you have the basics for all the fancy stitches you've seen and admired. Before you begin to knit, you need to have a few stitches on one knitting needle. The process of putting stitches on a needle is called casting on. But even before you cast on, you need a slip knot.

SLIP KNOT: Pull the strand of yarn from the skein until it measures about 36 inches. Approximately 18 inches from the free end of your yarn, make a slip knot as follows:

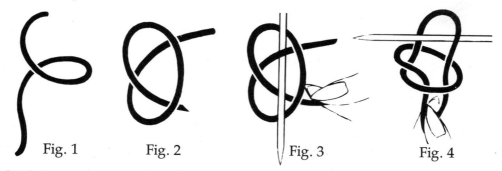

Fig. 1   Fig. 2   Fig. 3   Fig. 4

With the yarn, form a loop (Fig. 1). Lay the top strand of yarn under the loop (Fig. 2) and pull it through the loop with the tip of the knitting needle (Fig. 3 & 4), which is held in your right hand. Tighten the knot by pulling up with the needle while holding both ends of yarn in your left hand.

The slip knot is complete. Now you are ready to cast on.

CASTING ON

One-Needle Method

Fig. 1
Drape the free end of yarn over your left thumb and drape ball end of yarn over your left forefinger.

Fig. 2
Next, close the three remaining fingers of your left hand over both strands of yarn in your left palm. At this point you will be holding the needle with the point up in your right hand.

Fig. 3
Holding the yarn securely, pull the needle toward you and down. As you do this, a loop is formed on your thumb. Insert tip of needle under front of thumb loop.

Fig. 4
Then pass tip of needle over the top and under the yarn on the forefinger. Pull through thumb loop.

Fig. 5
Slip thumb out of loop and return thumb to original position. Pull stitch tight by spreading thumb and forefinger.

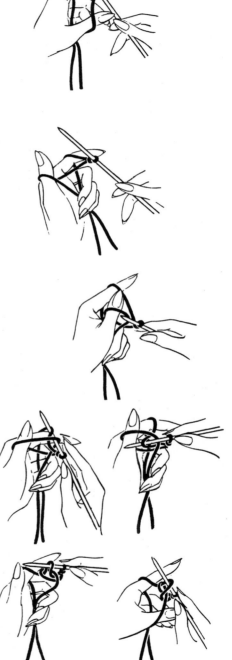

Repeat these steps until there are 20 stitches on the needle. This is the first row of your practice swatch. With this method of casting on, you need to determine the amount of yarn needed for the number of stitches. To do this, loosely wind the yarn around the needles the same number of times as there will be stitches. Add 5 or 6 more turns before making the slip knot, which counts as the first stitch.

Two-Needle Methods

The **knit-on** cast-on begins with a slip knot on the left needle. Insert right needle through slip knot from front to back. With right hand, wrap yarn around back of right needle, then to the front between the needles, gently pulling the yarn down into space between needles. Drop the tip of the right needle down and in front of the left needle, drawing the yarn through to the front. Slip loop in right needle onto left needle. Continue, always inserting right needle into last loop on left needle.

The **cable cast-on** is very similar to the knit-on method. However, you must start with 2 loops on the left needle. Insert right needle *between* the 2 loops, wrap yarn around right needle and draw through to the front. Place this loop on left needle.

Two-needle methods are especially useful when you are casting on in the middle or at the end of a row. At the end of a row, turn your work and cast on the beginning of the next row.

Abbreviations: In the instructions, abbreviations will be gradually introduced. You will notice after "Knit stitch," there is a k in parenthesis. K is the abbreviation for the knit stitch. A complete list of all knit and crochet abbreviations will be found on page 11 and 12.

Knit stitch (k): Using any of the methods given, cast on 20 stitches. Hold the needle with the stitches in your left hand. In your right hand, hold the other needle and the yarn that comes from the ball. The yarn needs to be held taut for proper tension. There is no "right" way to do this. Some people wrap it over the index finger and around the little finger. Others wrap it over their middle finger, then back over the index finger. This is simply a matter of what feels right for you. As you work, you will develop the proper tension and a comfortable position.

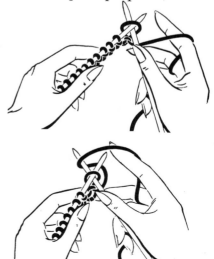

Fig. 1
Insert tip of right-hand needle from front to back of first stitch on left-hand needle.

Fig. 2
With index finger of right hand, guide yarn behind tip of right-hand needle and over front of right-hand needle, gently pulling the yarn down into space between needles.

Fig. 3
Next, pull right-hand needle down and in front of left-hand needle.

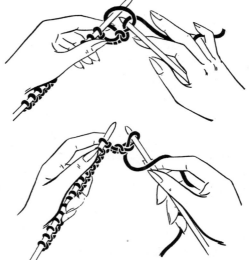

Fig. 4
With right-hand needle, push stitch off left-hand needle. Keep your left thumb and index finger on stitches not being worked.

Now you have completed one knit stitch. Keep repeating these steps until one row of knitting is completed. Don't become discouraged at this point! With a little practice, this whole awkward, jerky process will become natural and free-flowing. The first row of knitting after casting on is the most difficult even for the expert. Each row will seem easier. As with most things, practice will improve your skills.

When all 20 stitches are knit, reverse the position of your needles so that the needle with the stitches is in your left hand. Now knit another row just as you did the last one. Be sure you have 20 stitches after each row. Keep knitting until your practice swatch is about 4 inches.

The swatch you have just finished is called **garter stitch.** This is the easiest of all stitches—just knit each stitch on each row.

Purl stitch (p): The purl stitch is the other basic stitch necessary to knit. Actually, it is the reverse side of the knit stitch.

Fig. 1
Hold the needles just as you would to knit, but hold the yarn to the front of your work. Insert tip of right-hand needle into the front of the stitch on the left-hand needle.

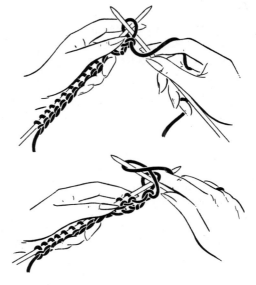

Fig. 2
Bring yarn over top of right-hand needle to the front.

Fig. 3
Pull right-hand needle tip back
and behind left-hand tip.

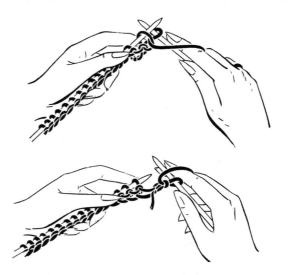

Fig. 4
Gently pull stitch off needle.

Repeat these steps on each stitch on this row. Now you have completed a purl row! Work several rows of purl stitch. Knit the next row. From now on, you will knit on the right side, which is smooth, and purl on the wrong side, which is bumpy. By alternating knit and purl rows, you will be working **stockinette stitch (St st).** Work until your swatch measures 4 inches, ending with the completion of a purl row.

Increasing (inc): When directions just say increase without specific information about how to do this, you would usually use the method known as **knit in the front and back of a stitch.**

Fig. 1   Fig. 2   Fig. 3

Starting at the beginning of a right-side row, knit the first 4 stitches as usual. Then in the next stitch, follow the first three steps of the knit stitch; that is, insert the tip of the right-hand needle as usual, wrap yarn around and pull yarn through to front, but do NOT push stitch off needle (Fig. 1). Instead, pull the right-hand needle toward you to loosen the stitch somewhat (Fig. 2); then put the right-hand needle behind left-hand needle and insert tip of needle into the **back** of the same stitch. Now, wrap yarn around needle again and this time complete the knit stitch (Fig. 3). You have added one stitch.

Knit 4 stitches before you work a **yarn over (yo),** often used in lacy patterns. A yarn over leaves a hole, so do not use this method unless your directions call for it.

Since you are working a knit row, your yarn is being held in back of the work. To make a yarn over before a knit stitch, bring the yarn to the front as if you were going to purl, but go right ahead and knit the next stitch. You will now have an extra loop on the right-hand needle.

Knit 4 stitches after the yarn over. Sometimes a pattern directs you to work a yarn over between a knit stitch and a purl stitch. To work this yarn over, bring the yarn between the needles to the front, over the right-hand needle to the back, then to the front again to purl. Purl the next 2 stitches; then, knit to the end of the row.

If you have made your increases correctly, you will now have 23 stitches on the needle. Purl all stitches on the next row, including the extra strands that were created by the yarn overs. Repeat these 2 rows until you are completely familiar with the increase methods. You will notice that holes appear where you made the yarn over increases, and that a small bump shows on the right side where you knit in the front and back of the same stitch.

Decreasing (dec):

On the next right-side row, knit a few stitches, then decrease a stitch by **knitting 2 stitches together (k2tog).** This is done by inserting the right-hand

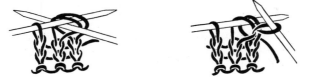

needle through 2 stitches on the left-hand needle, and knitting them as if they were one stitch.

Knit a few more stitches and then try a different decrease. This one is called **slip 1, knit 1, pass slip stitch over (sl 1, k1, psso).**

Fig. 1
Insert the tip of your right-hand needle into the next stitch on the left-hand needle as if you were going to knit it, but just pass it from the left to right needle without knitting it. You have just slipped a stitch (sl 1). Knit the next stitch (k 1).

Fig. 2
Now, insert the tip of the left-hand needle into the front of the slipped stitch and pull it over the knitted stitch and off the right-hand needle.

Work several rows, practicing these decreases until you again have 20 stitches on the needle.

Ribbing: On the next row of your sample swatch, work a few rows of knit 2, purl 2 ribbing, frequently used for waistbands, neck bands and cuffs. On the next row, knit 2 stitches, bring yarn between needles to front of work and purl 2 stitches; bring yarn between needles to back of work and knit 2 stitches; bring yarn to front of work and purl 2 stitches. Keep repeating these steps until a row is completed. On the next row, knit the knit stitches as they face you and purl the purl stitches. **Remember: yarn to back when knitting, yarn to front when purling!**

Another method of ribbing is to knit 1 and purl 1 alternately across the row.

Work a few rows in stockinette stitch to make binding off easier for your first attempt.

Binding off: When you complete a piece of knitting, you must have a finished edge that will not ravel. This is achieved by "binding off." Most beginners bind off too tightly. Keep your bound-off stitches as loose as possible. Knit the first 2 stitches from the left-hand needle to the right-hand needle. Slip the first stitch over the second stitch just as you did in the sl 1, k1, psso decrease. When you come to a purl stitch, you do basically the same thing with one small difference. Purl the stitch as usual, then bring the yarn to the back of your work as you slip one stitch over the other. Always remember to bring yarn to front to purl, take yarn to back to knit. Continue across row.

An alternative bind off can be worked by replacing the right-hand needle with a crochet hook. Knit the first 2 stitches. There will be 2 stitches on the hook. Pull the stitch nearest the hook through the other stitch. One stitch remains on hook. Continue across row, knitting knit stitches and purling purl stitches.

When there is just one stitch left, cut the yarn a few inches from the last stitch. Pull yarn through loop; pull tight to fasten off.

Crocheting

Crocheting, like knitting, has a few basic stitches. After you have learned to chain and work a single crochet, the rest are just variations. To begin, you will need a ball of worsted-weight yarn and a size G crochet hook.

Fig. 1   Fig. 2   Fig. 3

Slip knot: Hold the yarn near the end with the forefinger and thumb of your left hand. With your right hand, lap the yarn coming from the ball over the short end, holding loop in place with your thumb and forefinger (Fig. 1).

Hold the hook in your right hand and insert it through the loop. Catch the yarn with the hook and draw it through the loop (Fig. 2). Tighten loop by pulling gently on both ends. The slip knot is complete (Fig. 3).

Wrap the yarn around the little finger of your left hand; let it pass over your ring finger, under your middle finger and over your index finger. Hold hook in your right hand in the same way you hold a pencil. As you crochet, you may find that you'll hold the hook and even the yarn differently. Some people prefer to hold the hook as you hold a mixing spoon. Many people hold the yarn in slightly different ways. Find the position that's easiest for you. The yarn should be at an even tension, not too tight but not too much slack, either.

Abbreviations will be introduced in the directions of the stitches. You will find the abbreviation in parentheses following the term.

Chain stitch (ch): The chain stitch is the basis of all crochet. It is the foundation row on which the entire afghan is worked, and it is also used as a stitch (st) in the pattern.

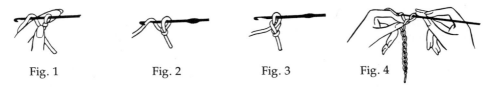

Fig. 1   Fig. 2   Fig. 3   Fig. 4

Pass the hook under the yarn that is lying over your index finger and catch the yarn with the hook. Pull this yarn through the loop on the hook. This makes 1 chain (ch). Keep repeating these steps until the chain is the desired length. For your practice piece, keep making chains until you can make them even and uniform in size. As you are working, it helps to keep your left thumb and forefinger close to the stitch you are working on. Tension is often a problem for beginners. Practice until it is natural and even.

Slip stitch (sl st): This stitch is used in joining or when an invisible stitch is needed. When directions say "join," use a slip stitch.

Fig. 1   Fig. 2

Insert hook from the front through 2 top strands of stitch (Fig 1). Yarn over and draw through stitch and loop on hook (Fig. 2).

Single crochet (sc): Make a foundation chain 4 to 5 inches long. As a general rule, your foundation chain should be worked looser than your other stitches. You may want to try using a hook one size larger when you work the beginning chain (ch).

Fig. 1   Fig. 2   Fig. 3   Fig. 4

Row 1: Insert hook under the 2 top strands of the second chain (ch) from the hook (Fig. 1). The chain (ch) on the hook is not counted. Skip the next chain and work into the second chain.

Catch the yarn with your hook and draw it through the chain. You now have 2 loops (lps) on the hook (Fig. 2). Yarn over, that is, pass the hook under the yarn and catch the yarn with the hook (Fig. 3). Draw the yarn through the 2 loops (lps) in one motion (Fig 4). You have now made 1 single crochet (sc).

Keep repeating these steps, making a single crochet (sc) in each chain to the end of the row. Remember to keep holding the chain with the thumb and forefinger close to the stitch (st) you are working. Don't be discouraged if this first row seems difficult. The first row is the hardest for even experienced crocheters. After the last single crochet (sc) has been made, chain 1 stitch (st) and turn the work so the opposite side is now facing you. Always work the row from right to left.

Row 2: Beginning in the first stitch (which is the last single crochet of the previous row), make 1 single crochet (sc) in each stitch (st) across the row, always passing the hook under the 2 top strands of the stitch unless specifically directed to do otherwise. End each row of single crochet by making a chain after the last single crochet. Repeat Row 2 at least 4 or 5 times, until you feel confident with the single crochet.

You will notice that each stitch from now on will be a little higher and longer than the previous stitch.

Half double crochet (hdc): If you are working this stitch on a foundation chain, chain 20 and work into the third chain from the hook. If you are working half double crochets onto the practice swatch you have already started, you will need to chain 2 at the end of the last row worked. The chain-2 will count as the first half double crochet (hdc).

Fig. 1   Fig. 2   Fig. 3

Wrap the yarn once around the hook and then insert the hook under the top 2 strands of the stitch. Wrap the yarn around and draw it through (Fig. 1). There are now 3 loops (lps) on the hook. Wrap the yarn around once more (Fig. 2) and draw it through all 3 loops (lps) on the hook (Fig. 3).

Continue working half double crochets (hdc) across the row. At the end of the row, chain 2 for the turning chain. Practice until you feel comfortable with the half double crochet.

Double crochet (dc): The double crochet is one of the most commonly used stitches (sts). If you are starting your double crochet on a foundation chain, you will work into the fourth chain from the hook. If you are continuing on your practice swatch, you will need to chain 3 at the end of the last row. This chain-3 will count as your first double crochet, and you will work a double crochet into the next stitch.

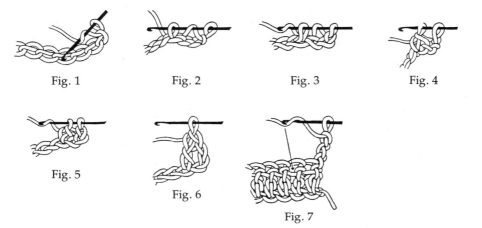

Fig. 1   Fig. 2   Fig. 3   Fig. 4

Fig. 5   Fig. 6   Fig. 7

Row 1: Wrap the yarn once around the hook (called a yarn over) and insert the hook under the top 2 strands of the stitch (st) (Fig. 1). Catch the yarn with the hook and draw it through the stitch (Fig 2). You now have 3 loops on the hook. Catch the yarn with the hook (yarn over) (Fig.3) and draw it through 2 of the 3 loops on the hook (Fig. 4). You now have 2 loops on the hook. Yarn over once more (Fig. 5) and draw the yarn through the last 2 loops on the hook. You now have 1 loop on the hook and have completed the double crochet (dc). Repeat these steps, working double crochet across the row. End each row by working 3 chains. Start each new row by working into the second stitch of the previous row (Fig 7). The turning chain counts as the first double crochet.

Post stitch: Any stitch can be worked as a post stitch, although the double crochet post stitch seems to be the most common. Normally, a stitch is worked into the top, horizontal part of the stitch in the row below. A post stitch is worked exactly like the regular stitch except it is worked around the post, the vertical, upright part of the stitch. To work a front post stitch, you insert the hook from the front around the back and to the front again. Continue to work the stitch as usual.

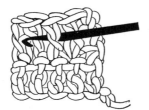
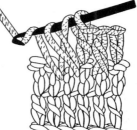

Treble crochet (tr): If you are starting your treble crochet on a foundation chain, work into the fifth chain from the hook. If you are working on your practice swatch, chain 4 and count the turning chain as the first treble.

Wrap the yarn twice around the hook before inserting the hook into the second stitch of the row below. Yarn over and draw the yarn through. There are now 4 loops on the hook.

Yarn over and draw yarn through 2 loops. Three loops remain. Yarn over again and draw through 2 loops. Complete the stitch by yarning over and drawing through 2 loops once more. At the end of the row, chain 4 for the turning chain, which as before, will count as the first treble crochet (tr).

Double treble crochet (dtr): On a foundation chain, this stitch is started in the sixth chain from the hook. The yarn is wrapped three times around the hook and drawn through 2 loops at a time until only one loop remains. Chain 5 to turn your work.

To turn your work: In crochet, at the end of the row, a certain number of chain stitches is added to bring work into position for the next row. Work is then turned so that the reverse side is facing you. The number of turning chains depends on the stitch the next row begins with. Your directions will tell you how many to chain before you turn. The turning chain always counts as the first stitch except in single crochet. With single crochet, the chain-1 only raises the work to position, but does not usually count as the first stitch.

To join new yarn and change colors: Hold new yarn along top of row and work over it for several inches. When near the end of the old yarn, draw new yarn through last 2 loops of final stitch, then continue with new yarn, working over the end of old yarn for several inches. When joining a new color, draw the new color through last 2 loops of final step of the stitch. Continue with new color, working over end of old yarn for several inches. Weave any ends in back of work with crochet hook or large-eyed yarn needle.

Ending or fastening off: Cut the yarn about 4 to 5 inches from the last stitch. Pull the loose end through the loop on the hook. Pull the loose end tight and weave it into the back of your stitches.

How to increase (inc): Work 2 stitches in one stitch to add an extra stitch.

How to decrease (dec): Single crochet: Work a single crochet to the point where 2 loops are left on the hook. Insert hook from the front under the 2 top strands of the next stitch. Yarn over and draw through stitch. There are now 3 loops on the hook (Fig. 1).

Fig. 1   Fig. 2

Yarn over and draw through 3 loops at once (Fig. 2). You have worked 2 single crochet together (tog) and there is 1 less stitch on the row.

Double crochet: Work a double crochet (dc) to the point where there are 2 loops on the hook. Yarn over (yo) and insert hook from front under 2 top strands of next stitch (Fig. 1). Yarn over and through 1 loop. There are 4 loops on hook. Yarn over again and through 2 loops. There are 3 loops on hook (Fig. 2). Yarn over and through 3 loops (Fig. 3). You have worked 2 double crochet together and have 1 less stitch on the row.

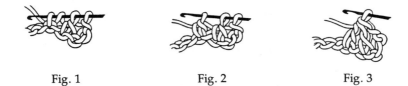

Fig. 1   Fig. 2   Fig. 3

Finishing

After spending hours, weeks and maybe months on an afghan, you don't want to ruin the wonderful handmade look. Some patterns tell you how to finish your seams, make fringe or tassels. Embroidery stitches that are used are sometimes included. But sometimes more complete instructions for finishing are needed.

BLOCKING can be done in several ways and sometimes shouldn't be done at all. Many of the synthetics should not be blocked. Check the label on your yarn.

Some experts think each piece should be blocked before the seams are worked. Others sew the seams and then block. Often the seams are easier to work after blocking.

The traditional way of blocking is to pin the piece to the correct measurements and then steam it by holding a steam iron just above, but never actually touching the fabric. Wool yarns can be safely blocked this way.

A damp cloth or towel can be placed on the piece. Then iron, keeping the weight of the iron off the fabric, just barely touching the damp towel.

Another popular method is to pin the piece to a sturdy surface that has been covered with a cloth. A piece of cardboard covered with a towel works fine. With rustproof pins, pin at 1-inch intervals. Fill a clean spray bottle with water and spray your knit or crocheted fabric until it is evenly damp but not soaked. Leave on the blocking surface until totally dry.

An alternative to both these methods is to wash the completed afghan following care instructions from the yarn label, or just dampen the afghan between towels. Then pat into shape and let dry.

SEAMS: If the instructions do not tell you what seam to use, any of these seams will work. With any seam, do not work too tight. The seam should have the same amount of "give" as the finished afghan. Line up the pieces carefully, so all patterns and stripes will match.

Weaving is the preferred way to work a straight seam. It produces a seam with very little bulk. Lay the two pieces to be joined, right sides up, with edges touching one another. Thread a yarn needle (blunt point and large-eyed) with the same yarn used in the afghan. If the yarn is thick, separate the strands for a finer thread. Insert the needle through the center of the first stitch on the piece on your right. Draw the yarn up through the stitch above it. Then, insert the needle through the center of the first stitch of the left piece and draw the yarn up through the stitch above it. After the first set of stitches is completed, repeat the same process, but passing under two rows of knitting each time, being sure not to pull too tight.

If you prefer crocheting, work a **slip stitch** seam. This seam may be bulky. Pin the two pieces together with right sides facing each other. There are now pins on the market that are long and blunt just for this purpose. Some people prefer the plastic picks that are used with hair rollers. Do not use anything with a sharp point that will split the yarn. With a ball of yarn and a crochet hook, pull a loop through both thicknesses. Insert the hook through the next row of stitches and draw through another loop. There are now 2 loops on the hook. Draw the loop nearest the hook end through the other loop on the hook, completing a slip stitch. Repeat this procedure, pulling the loop from the back through the fabric and loop on the needle in one motion, to the end of the pieces.

Back stitch: Pin right sides together. Bring tapestry needle threaded with yarn through to front; work one stitch to the right (or backwards). Bring needle up to left of last stitch. Insert needle back down into same spot as previous stitch started, coming up to left of last stitch.

Overcast stitch: Pin right sides together. Insert needle behind the knot of the edge stitch, then into the same part of the stitch on the corresponding row of the other piece. Pull yarn through and repeat to end of seam, working behind the knot rather than through it for a strong seam. This will make a flat seam if you do not work into the entire edge stitch.

FRINGE is often worked on the ends of the afghan. Cut a piece of cardboard the desired length of the fringe. Wrap the yarn around the cardboard many times. Cut along one edge of the cardboard. Taking 1, 2, 3 or 4 strands (pattern should indicate how many) of yarn together, fold them in half. With a crochet hook from the back, pull the folded part through to the back. Then take the ends and pull them through the loop. This will put the folded part facing the front.

TASSELS are sometimes worked instead of fringe, often on the corners of an afghan. Cut a piece of cardboard the same length as the finished tassel. Cut one piece of yarn about 6 inches long; hold along top edge of cardboard. Wrap the yarn around the cardboard over this strand of yarn, continuing until the yarn is the desired thickness for a tassel. Tie the 6-inch strand of yarn to hold the tassel together. This will be the top of the tassel. Remove the cardboard and pull the tied strand tight; tie several knots. The ends will be used to fasten the tassel to the afghan. Take another strand of yarn and tie around the tassel about 1 inch from the top. Hide the ends in the tassel. Cut the yarn at the bottom; trim and attach.

EMBROIDERY STITCHES are often used to decorate an afghan. The most common stitches used are the chain stitch, lazy daisy and French knots.

Chain stitch: Bring needle to right side of fabric. Hold thread down with thumb. Insert needle as close as possible to spot where thread emerges, bring out a short distance below. Draw needle through over loop.

Lazy daisy: A loop is formed with yarn while needle is inserted into the same hole where the yarn first emerged from cloth. Hold loop down with thumb of left hand while sewing a stitch. The needle passes over looped yarn. The loop is then held in place by a small stitch sewn over the center of the loop.

French knots: Bring needle up at point where knot is to be made. Wind yarn 2 or 3 times around point of needle; insert in fabric as close as possible to spot where yarn emerged, but not in exact spot. Pull to wrong side, holding twists in place.

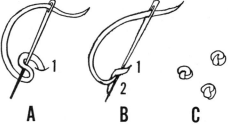

A   B   C

Just because the knitting or crocheting is done, don't rush through the finishing. Take your time and do a good job. Finishing can make the difference between a beautiful handmade afghan and a homemade afghan!

Conversion Charts

Crochet Hook Size Conversion

Metric (mm)	U.S. size	English
2¼	B-1	13
2¾	C-2	12
3¼	D-3	10
3½	E-4	—
3¾	F-5	9
4¼	G-6	—
4½	7	7
5	H-8	6
5½	I-9	5
6	J-10	4
6½	K-10½	3
7	—	2
8	L-11	—
9	M-13	—
10	N-15	—
11½	P-16	—
16	Q	—
19	S	—

Knitting Needle Size Conversion

Metric (mm)	U.S. size	English
2	0	14
2¼	1	13
2¾	2	12
3	—	11
3¼	3	10
3½	4	—
3¾	5	9
4	—	8
4¼	6	—
4½	7	7
5	8	6
5¼	—	—
5½	9	5
5¾	—	—
6	10	4
6½	10½	3
7	—	2
7½	—	1
8	11	0
9	13	00
10	15	000
12¾	17	—
15	19	—
19	35	—
25	50	—

Ounces to Grams Conversion

¼ ounce	=	7.08 grams
½ ounce	=	14.18 grams
¾ ounce	=	21.26 grams
1 ounce	=	28.26 grams
2 ounces	=	56.70 grams
3 ounces	=	85.05 grams
3½ ounces	=	100.00 grams
4 ounces	=	114.18 grams

Grams to Ounces

1 gram	=	.035 ounce
50 grams	=	1.75 ounces
100 grams	=	3.5 ounces

Instructions

At the beginning of each pattern, you will see that the patterns are rated easy, intermediate or advanced. The ratings were determined by the complexity of the pattern and the stitches used. This should help you to choose a pattern for your skill level.

In the instructions, colors are referred to as A, B, C, etc. to encourage you to choose colors pleasing to you. The actual colors used for the afghan as pictured are given in the Materials section of each pattern. Specific color names are not given because of the wide variety of names used by the yarn companies. Choose colors to complement your decor.

The symbol at the beginning of each pattern will clearly indicate whether the afghan is knit or crocheted.

Cardinal Afghan

SIZE: approximately 43 × 58 inches.

MATERIALS: worsted-weight yarn (220 yards per skein): 6 skeins color A (ecru); 2 skeins color B (red); 1 skein each of the following: color C (dark red), color D (dark brown heather), color E (light brown heather), color F (dark green heather) and color G (light green heather); 40 yards color H (black) and 5 yards color I (gold). Crochet hook size I or size required to achieve recommended gauge; yarn bobbins.

GAUGE: 7 sts = 2 inches
3 rows = 1 inch

Be sure to check your gauge before starting. Use any size hook that will give the correct stitch gauge. If your gauge is not correct or if you make adjustments in the size of the afghan, the yarn amounts may not be sufficient.

Work the center of the afghan first. The cardinal and trees are crocheted following the chart. Border will be added after the center is complete.

AFGHAN: Ch 85.

Row 1: Hdc in 3rd ch from hook and in each ch across—84 hdc. Ch 2, turn.
Note: Starting with next row, do *not* count turning ch as first hdc. Do *not* work into turning ch. Ch 2 at end of each row. There will be 84 sts in each row of center section.
Row 2: Hdc in first hdc and in each hdc across—84 hdc. Ch 2, turn.
Rows 3–23: Repeat Row 2. Afghan should measure approximately 8 inches.

To work with colors: Bobbins of each color will be added as the color is needed. Bobbins will eliminate some of the tangles that would occur with the entire balls of yarn. When the color is no longer needed, cut the yarn and bobbin off leaving a 3–4-inch strand. Weave strand in back. *Always* carry the bobbin on wrong side of yarn. If you carry more than 3 or 4 stitches, twist the bobbin yarn around color being worked to prevent long, loose strands on the wrong side.

When changing colors, pull new color through on last step of half double crochet; that is, when there are 3 loops on hook.

To work from chart: With right side of afghan facing you, begin at lower right corner of chart. Work chart from bottom to top. Right-side rows (even-numbered rows) are worked from right to left. Wrong-side rows (odd-numbered rows) are worked from left to right. Work colors as indicated by symbols.
Row 24: (first row of chart) Work 12 hdc, then follow 60 sts as shown on chart (working right to left), work 12 hdc to end of row—84 sts.

Continue to work entire chart, always working the 12 hdc at each side. When chart is complete, work 23 rows hdc in A, changing to B in last st of last row. Do *not* fasten off.

Border: *Rnd 1:* With right side facing and B, sc around, working 2 sc in first row, sc down left side, working 1 sc in each row, 3 sc in corner; 1 sc in each st across bottom, 3 sc in corner; 1 sc in each row of right side, 3 sc in corner; sc in each st across, working last sc in same sp as first 2 sc were worked. Ch 1, turn.
Rnd 2: With B, sc in front lp only around afghan, working 3 sc in center st of each corner. Fasten off.
Rnd 3: Join A with sl st in any center corner st, ch 6, dc in same st, ch 1, 2 dc in next st. * (Ch 1, skip one st, 2 dc in next st) to corner. Dc, ch 3, dc in center corner st. Repeat from * to beg

☐ Ecru	☒ Dark brown heather	⊟ Light green heather
⊡ Red	⊠ Light brown heather	◪ Black
◿ Dark red	⊞ Dark green heather	⊙ Gold

of rnd. Sl st to 3rd ch of ch-6.

Rnd 4: Sl st to center ch of corner. Then, repeat Rnd 3, working the 2 dc in ch-1 of previous rnd.

Rnds 5 & 6: Repeat Rnd 4.

Rnd 7: With E, repeat Rnd 4 but do *not* work ch-1 between 2 dc. *Note:* Do **not** work ch-1 on any following rnds.

Rnd 8: With D, repeat Rnd 7, working 2 dc between 2-dc groups of previous rnd.

Rnds 9,10,11: With A, repeat Rnd 8.

Rnds 12 & 13: With G, repeat Rnd 8.

Rnds 14,15,16: With F, repeat Rnd 8.

Rnd 17: With F, work 1 rnd of reverse single crochet around entire afghan. Fasten off.

Reverse single crochet: Work single crochet, working from left to right. Be sure to pull up a loop long enough to work.

Optional: You may want to work a piece the same size as the center panel if the back of the cardinal and the trees have long loose strands. With B, attach around outer edge of panel. Yarn amounts for this back panel have *not* been included in materials.

Monk's Cloth Afghan

Shown on page 33

Even if you can't knit or crochet, you can make this afghan, using Swedish weaving and monk's cloth. Swedish weaving is a type of surface embroidery more commonly worked with embroidery floss on huck cloth or huck toweling. Although the weave and texture of monk's cloth is quite different, the techniques are the same. A simple offset stitch, one of several common stitches, is used on our monk's cloth afghan to produce a ripple design.

There is one term that may be new to you. Throughout the directions, you will see the word "float." On monk's cloth, a float consists of four adjoining threads. You will be passing the threaded needle under vertical floats and over horizontal floats. The chart shows only the vertical floats for ease in following directions.

SIZE: Directions are for one 60-×-72-inch afghan or one 36-×-60-inch lap robe and two 15-inch square pillows.

MATERIALS: 2 yards of 60-inch-wide monk's cloth, worsted-weight acrylic yarn (230 yards per skein): 3 skeins color A, 2 skeins color B, 1 skein color C and 1 skein color D. Tapestry needle size 14, 16 or 18.

GENERAL DIRECTIONS: To be sure that your design is balanced, always start in the center and work one row from center to left edge. Then start again at the center and work row to the right edge.

It is very important that you work loosely so that your stitches lie flat and smooth. Do not pull the yarn tight at any time!

AFGHAN

Preparation: Before you do anything else, turn under and machine-stitch a ½-inch hem on all cut edges. Turn selvage edge under and sew in place. This is extremely important as monk's cloth ravels quite easily.

Do not launder until afghan is completed. The shrinking that occurs during the first laundering will tighten the stitches and give a firmer finish.

Cutting yarn: As a general rule, you will need a strand of yarn 2½ times the width of the fabric to complete 1 row. With 60-inch monk's cloth, this means that it will take approximately 5 yards to work 1 row. Cut the yarn carefully to avoid waste. As you work, you may find you can cut a little less than 5 yards for each row.

Working direction: Swedish weaving is usually worked from right to left with the first row started in the center. When the left half of that first row is finished, turn work upside down and turn chart upside down, then complete right half to match left half.

To start: Fold fabric in half from top to bottom (with selvages at either side). This will give you the horizontal center of the fabric. Keeping this fold in place, fold fabric in half in other direction for the vertical center of the fabric. The point where the folds meet is the exact center of your fabric. Mark the center with a pin.

Color pattern: Color sequence is 5 rows A, 1 row D, 4 rows B, 1 row D, 3 rows C, 1 row D.
Since the first (center) row is worked in A, the next 2 rows are worked in A, next row is D, next 4 rows B, 1 row D, 3 rows C, 1 row D, then 5 rows A, and repeat sequence.

Following the design chart: Each double vertical line on chart represents ONE float. One float equals 4 adjoining threads. Thread a tapestry

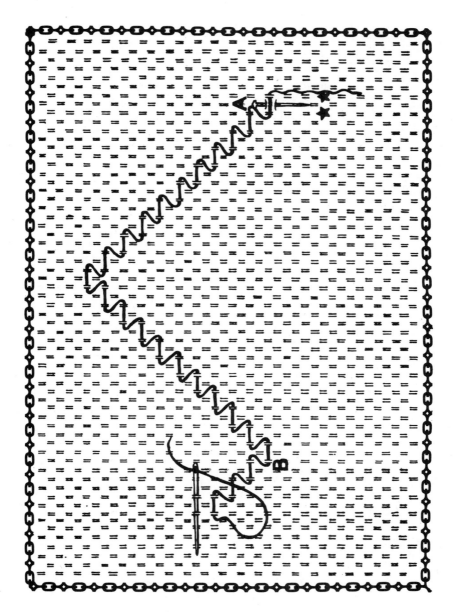

needle with 5 yards of color A. When you have found the exact center of your fabric, start at that point by passing the threaded needle under 2 floats at the point marked by A on chart, letting half of the yarn hang free below that point. You will be working from the center of chart and fabric to the left edge. (At this point, ignore the 2 stars shown below the drawing of the pin on chart.)

After passing under the first 2 floats, bring needle up to the float just above

the vertical float where the previous weaving stitch ended. Again, pass needle under 2 floats, thus moving up 1 step and over 1 step. Continue in this manner until you have completed 10 steps. Now you will be stepping down, starting the next stitch by passing needle under the float just below the float where the previous stitch ended. Make the same number of downward steps and then start up again, repeating from A to B across until you reach the left edge of the fabric.

When this is done, turn fabric upside down and work to other edge in same manner. **Every row is worked in this same manner.**

For the 2nd row: Thread needle with color A and start at point marked with 2 stars on the chart. *Work exactly like Row 1.* Continue working in this manner, following directions for color pattern sequence until lower edge of afghan is reached. At top and bottom of afghan, you will not have space for full rows. Just fill in the spaces with the "peaks" of the pattern rows. When you have completed the pattern to the lower edge, turn afghan upside down and work to other end as before.

FINISHING: Conceal all loose ends in the selvage hem. You are now ready to use your afghan unless you would like to add an OPTIONAL CROCHETED BORDER. If you have some yarn left over and know how to crochet (see page 19 for single crochet directions), this adds a beautiful finishing touch. Starting with the light shade of yarn and a size G or H crochet hook, work 1 row of single crochet around all edges, spacing the stitches so you have approximately 4 stitches per inch. In each corner, make 3 stitches in the same space so the corners will lie flat. Work 4 more rows, working through back loop only, using the same color sequence as you used for weaving pattern WITHOUT the accent color (color D).

LAP ROBE

A lap robe can be made following the same directions and using 36 inches of material.

PILLOW

Any desired size pillow can be made to match your lap robe; cloth is needed to complete 2 pillow tops or the top and bottom of 1 pillow.

Cutting the fabric: It is the nature of monk's cloth to shrink when washed, and this tendency should be taken into consideration when cutting the fabric. It is best to work your design without prewashing the fabric, as shrinkage of the new fabric will tighten the weave, making it more difficult to do the weaving. Also, the measuring directions given below for starting design placement are based on unwashed fabric.

From unwashed monk's cloth, cut 1 piece 21-×-21 inches.

To start: Fold fabric in half from top to bottom, with selvage at the side. Mark center fold with a safety pin.

Work pattern as in pattern sequence of afghan until desired size. You can use a shorter length of yarn in the needle; 2½ yards should be ample.

If desired, make a pillow back in the same manner. Otherwise, cut a piece of 16-×-16-inch fabric for the backing.

FINISHING: If you plan to remove and wash the pillow cover, it is best to wash the woven piece before assembling into a pillow. Handle gently in lukewarm or cold water. BE SURE THAT ALL EDGES ARE SECURELY HEMMED SO THEY WILL NOT RAVEL WHEN WASHED.

Trim edges of woven piece(s) to measure 16 × 16 inches. Make a double row of machine stitches near outer edges of monk's cloth. Place pillow front and pillow backing together, having WRONG sides facing out. Pin so all edges and corners are even and join the 2 pieces along 3 edges with machine-stitching, using a ½-inch seam allowance. Turn so that right sides are facing out and insert a 15-x-15-inch pillow form or stuff with Polyfil. Turn under a ½-inch hem on remaining raw edges and whip together by hand.

CARE: Wash on gentle cycle with cool water. Tumble dry on gentle cycle with low to medium heat.

*E*ven if you can't knit or crochet, you can make this soft afghan using easy-to-learn Swedish weaving on monk's cloth. Directions on page 30.

*A*ran afghans are always a favorite. The knit version (below) is covered with cable variations. Popcorns and post stitches create the crocheted Aran look (top). Directions for knit Aran on page 51. Directions for crocheted Aran on page 49.

*D*ouble the yarn and cut your time in half.
Large needles and double strands of yarn
make this knit fisherman afghan warm and cozy.
Directions on page 55.

J oin four squares of pretty petals together to form
lovely knit flowers. This afghan comes in two
sizes, one full size (as shown) and a smaller
version for baby. Directions on page 56.

*T*he Lullaby afghan is worked in small squares with two colors. You can crochet a baby afghan as shown or a full-size afghan. A wonderful gift for a new baby—and Mom will love it, too. Directions on page 58.

*P*erfect for a picnic! This Indian blanket is great
in the outdoors or the den. Nine panels are
knit from easy-to-follow charts. Directions on
page 59.

*R*emember Grandma's Ripple afghan? Crochet
your own in four colors to complement your
decor. It always looks great! Directions on page 61.

*A*s soft as a kitten! This Quick Popcorn afghan
is so inviting. Crochet it with a bulky brushed
yarn and a large hook. Directions on page 62.

*D*iamonds are a girl's best friend—and these are also quick and easy to knit. Directions on page 63.

*D*elightful! This Pennsylvania Dutch afghan crocheted in bright colors will brighten any corner in your home. Worked in easy-to-take-along motifs! Directions on page 64.

*T*he man in your life will love this vibrant afghan. Horizontal stripes are knit in stockinette stitch. Dropped stitches create loose strands on which to crochet the vertical stripes. Directions on page 65.

*Y*ou'll love the texture of this bouncy Honeycomb knit stitch. Only two colors create all three shades of this geometric design. Directions on page 66.

*L*ooks hard but it is easy enough for a beginner's first crocheted afghan. Your friends will be impressed—and you'll be so proud! Directions on page 68.

*D*ream of sailing away? Set sail with this
wonderful crocheted nautical design.
Directions on page 69.

*M*idwinter blahs? Surround yourself with
*beautiful flowers from the tropics.
Embroider the brightly colored flowers in cross
stitch on the solid afghan stitch panels. Directions
on page 73.*

This is no blarney! Take your choice of a knit Irish Lace worked in panels or a crocheted Shamrock design worked in square motifs. Both have a formal, lacy look suitable for living room or bedroom. Directions for Irish Lace on page 79. Directions for Shamrocks on page 77.

Aran Crochet

Shown on page 34

SIZE: approximately 52 × 68 inches excluding fringe.

MATERIALS: worsted-weight yarn (230 yards per skein): 16 skeins. Crochet hook size H or size required to achieve recommended gauge.

GAUGE: 3 dc = 1 inch
2 rows = 1 inch

Be sure to check your gauge before starting. Use any size hook that will give the correct stitch gauge. If your gauge is not correct or if you make adjustments in the size of the afghan, the yarn amounts may not be sufficient.

Note: Post stitches are worked around the post (vertical upright part of the stitch). Post stitches in this pattern are all post treble stitches.

Front post treble stitch: (worked on right-side rows) Wrap yarn around hook twice, insert hook from front, behind the post and back to the front. Yarn over and draw through. (Yarn over and draw through 2 loops) 3 times.

Back post treble stitch: (worked on wrong-side rows) Wrap yarn around hook twice, insert hook from back of work, around front of post, back to position in back of work. Yarn over and draw through. (Yarn over and draw through 2 loops) 3 times.

Post stitch pattern: (worked on 13 stitches) (Treble post stitch, double crochet in next 2 stitches) 4 times, treble post stitch.

Popcorn: (worked on 1 stitch) Double crochet 5 times in next stitch, remove hook and insert in first double crochet of group, catch loop of last double crochet and draw through first double crochet, tighten stitch.

AFGHAN: (worked in 1 piece) Turning ch counts as first dc.

Ch 168 sts loosely. Dc in 3rd ch from hook and in each ch across—167 sts.

Note: Work front post sts on Rows 1, 3, 5 and 7 (right-side rows). Work back post sts on Rows 2, 4, 6 and 8 (wrong-side rows).

Row 1: (right-side row) Ch 3, post st pattern on next 13 sts, * dc in next 12 dc, popcorn in next st, dc in next 12 sts, post st pattern on next 13 sts. Repeat from * across, ending with dc in top of turning ch.
Row 2: (wrong-side row) Ch 3, post st pattern on next 13 sts, * dc in next 11 sts, popcorn in next st, dc in next st, popcorn in next st, dc in next 11 sts, post stitch pattern on next 13 sts. Repeat from * across, ending dc in top of turning ch.
Row 3: Ch 3, post st pattern on next 13 sts, * dc in next 10 sts, popcorn in next st, dc in next 3 sts, popcorn in next st, dc in next 10 sts, post st pattern on next 13 sts. Repeat from * across, ending dc in top of turning ch.
Row 4: Ch 3, post st pattern on next 13 sts, * dc in next 9 sts, popcorn in next st, dc in next 5 sts, popcorn in next st, dc in next 9 sts, post st pattern on next 13 sts. Repeat from * across, ending dc in top of turning ch.
Row 5: Ch 3, post st pattern on next 13 sts, * dc in next 8 sts, popcorn in next st, dc in next 3 sts, popcorn in next st, dc in next 3 sts, popcorn in next st, dc in next 8 sts, post st pattern on next 13 sts. Repeat from * across, ending dc in top of turning ch.
Row 6: Ch 3, post st pattern on next 13 sts, * dc in next 7 sts, popcorn in next st, dc in next 3 sts, popcorn in next st, dc in next st, popcorn in next st, dc in next 3 sts, popcorn in next st, dc in next 7 sts, post st pattern on next 13 sts. Repeat from * across, ending dc in top of turning ch.

Row 7: Ch 3, post st pattern on next 13 sts, * dc in next 6 sts, popcorn in next st, dc in next 3 sts, popcorn in next st, dc in next 3 sts, popcorn in next st, dc in next 3 sts, popcorn in next st, dc in next 6 sts, post st pattern on next 13 sts. Repeat from * across, ending dc in top of turning ch.

Row 8: Ch 3, post st pattern on next 13 sts, * dc in next 5 sts, popcorn in next st, dc in next 3 sts, popcorn in next st, dc in next 5 sts, popcorn in next st, dc in next 3 sts, popcorn in next st, dc in next 5 sts, post st pattern on next 13 sts. Repeat from * across, ending dc in top of turning ch.

Repeat Row 7, then Row 6, then Row 5, then Row 4, then Row 3, then Row 2 **. Beginning with Row 1, repeat the pattern to ** 9 times, then work Row 1 again. End with 1 row dc to match beginning.

Fringe: Knot 4 14-inch strands of yarn in between every 3rd dc across each end.

SIZE: approximately 45 × 54 inches excluding fringe

MATERIALS: worsted-weight yarn (230 yards per skein): 10 skeins. Cable needle, 29-inch circular needle size 10 or size required to achieve recommended gauge.

GAUGE: 4 sts = 1 inch in stockinette stitch. Gauges will be given for individual patterns.

Be sure to check your gauge before starting. Use any size needles that will give the correct stitch gauge. If your stitch gauge is not correct or if you make adjustments in the size of the afghan, the yarn amounts may not be sufficient.

Note: Afghan is made in 3 panels. In directions for each panel, you will be told to place markers on the needle. The markers will let you know when to change from one pattern to another. On following rows, always pass markers from left to right needle.

CENTER PANEL: (make 1) Cast on 120 sts.
Foundation Row: K1, work Foundation Row of Traveling Rib Pattern on next 34 sts, place marker on needle, k4, place marker; work Foundation Row of Ribbed Lattice Pattern on next 42 sts; place marker, k4, place marker; work Foundation Row of Traveling Rib Pattern on next 34 sts; k1.
Next Rows: Keeping first and last sts and the 4 sts between patterns in

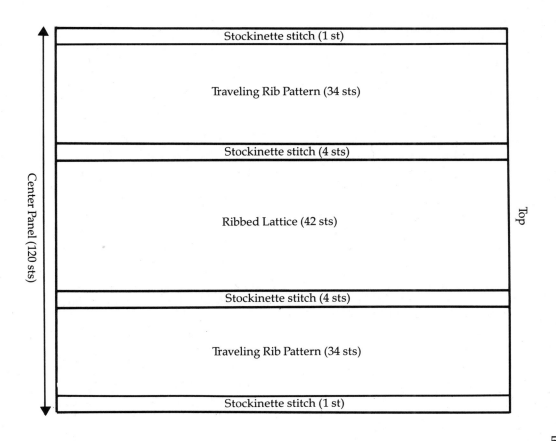

stockinette stitch, repeat the rows of each pattern between markers as established until Ribbed Lattice Pattern (with 24 rows in each repeat) has been repeated 13 times in all. Then work 3 more rows in all patterns. Bind off, knitting all knit sts and purling all purl sts.

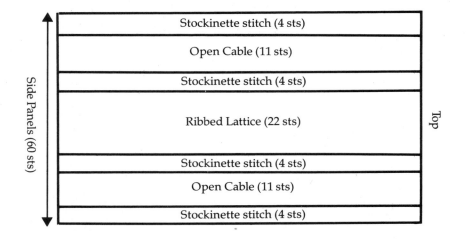

SIDE PANELS: (make 2) For each side panel, cast on 60 sts.

Foundation Row: K4, place marker; work Foundation Row of Open Cable on next 11 sts; place marker, k4, place marker; work Foundation Row of Ribbed Lattice on next 22 sts; place marker, k4, place marker; work Foundation Row of Open Cable on next 11 sts; place marker, k4.

Next Rows: Keeping the 4 sts at left edge of left panel (right edge of right panel) in garter st and the 4 sts between patterns and at other edge in St st, repeat the rows of each pattern between markers as established until Ribbed Lattice Pattern has been repeated 13 times in all. Then work 3 more rows of all patterns. Bind off, knitting all knit sts and purling all purl sts.

Pattern Stitches

TRAVELING RIB PATTERN: (multiple of 6 stitches plus 4) Pattern should measure 6 inches over 34 stitches. Used in center panels.

Cross 4: Slip 3 stitches to cable needle; hold in back. Knit 1, then holding yard in front, slip 2 purl stitches from cable needles back to left needle and purl them. Knit remaining stitch from cable needle.

Foundation Row: (right side) K1, * p2, k1; repeat from * 10 more times.

Rows 1 & 3: P1, * k2, p1; repeat from * 10 more times.

Row 2: K1, * p2, k1; repeat from * to end.

Row 4: * Cross 4, p2; repeat from * across, ending with Cross 4.

Rows 5, 6 & 7: Repeat Rows 1,2,3.

Row 8: K1, p2, * Cross 4, p2; repeat from * across, ending with k1. Repeat Rows 1–8 for pattern. (Do not repeat Foundation Row.)

RIBBED LATTICE WITH BOBBLES: (multiple of 20 stitches plus 2; worked on 22 stitches for side panels, 42 stitches for center panel) Pattern should measure 4 inches over 22 stitches. Used on center and side panels.

Knit through back loop (k tbl): Insert right needle tip into back of loop on left needle instead of into front of loop.

Purl through back loop (p tbl): Position right needle tip at back of stitches

52

on left needle tip, between the first and 2nd stitches. Now, insert needle tip from left to right through the back of the first stitch and purl from this position.

Back Cross: Slip 1 stitch to cable needle and hold in back of work; knit 1 in back loop; then, purl 1 from cable needle.

Front Cross: Slip 1 stitch to cable needle and hold in front, purl 1; then, knit 1 in back loop from cable needle.

Bobble: Work on 4 stitches as follows: (Knit 4, turn work to opposite side; purl 4, turn work to opposite side.) Repeat between parentheses 2 more times. Right side of work is now facing you. Then pick up a loop from first row of bobble and knit it together with first stitch on left needle; knit 2, then pick up a loop from first row of bobble and knit it together with next stitch, completing bobble.

Foundation Row: (right side) P6, * (k1 tbl, p1) twice, k2 tbl, (p1, k1 tbl) twice, p10; repeat from * across, ending last repeat with p6 instead of p10.
Row 1: K6, * (p1 tbl, k1) twice, p2 tbl, (k1, p1 tbl) twice, k10; repeat from * across, ending last repeat with k6 instead of k10.
Row 2: P6, * k1 tbl, p1, k1 tbl; on next 4 sts work a bobble; k1 tbl, p1, k1 tbl, p10; repeat from * across, ending last repeat with p6 instead of p10.
Row 3: K6, * (p1 tbl, k1) twice, p2 tbl, (k1, p1 tbl) twice, k10; repeat from * across, ending last repeat with k6 instead of k10.
Row 4: P5, * work Back Cross 3 times, work Front Cross 3 times, p8; repeat from * across, ending last repeat with p5 instead of p8.
*Row 5 and all remaining **wrong**-side rows except Row 15:* K all k sts and p tbl all p sts.
Row 6: P4, * work Back Cross 3 times, p2, work Front Cross 3 times, p6; repeat from * across, ending last repeat with p4 instead of p6.
Row 8: P3, * work Back Cross 3 times,

p4, work Front Cross 3 times, p4; repeat from *, ending last repeat with p3 instead of p4.
Row 10: P2, * work Back Cross 3 times, p6, work Front Cross 3 times, p2; repeat from * across.
Row 12: P1, * work Back Cross 3 times, p8, work Front Cross 3 times; repeat from *, ending with p1.
Row 14: (side panels only) P1, bobble on next 4 sts, k1 tbl, p10, k1 tbl, bobble on next 4 sts, p1—22 sts.
Row 14: (center panel only) P1, bobble on next 4 sts, k1 tbl, p10, k1 tbl, p1, k1 tbl, bobble on next 4 sts, k1 tbl, p1, k1 tbl, p10, k1 tbl, bobble on next 4 sts, p1—42 sts.
Row 15: (wrong side) K1, * (p1 tbl, k1) twice, p1 tbl, k10, (p1 tbl, k1) twice, p1 tbl; repeat from * across, ending with k1.
Row 16: P1, * work Front Cross 3 times, p8, work Back Cross 3 times; repeat from * across, ending with p1.
Row 18: P2, * work Front Cross 3 times, p6, work Back Cross 3 times, p2; repeat from * across.
Row 20: P3, * work Front Cross 3 times, p4, work Back Cross 3 times, p4; repeat from * across, ending last repeat with p3, instead of p4.
Row 22: P4, * work Front Cross 3 tmes, p2, work Back Cross 3 times, p6; repeat from * across, ending last repeat with p4 instead of p6.
Row 24: P5, * work Front Cross 3 times, work Back Cross 3 times, p8; repeat from * across, ending last repeat with p5 instead of p8.
Repeat Rows 1–24 for pattern. (Do not repeat Foundation Row.)

OPEN CABLE PATTERN: (worked on 11 stitches) Pattern should measure 2 inches across 11 stitches. Used on side panels.

Cross back: Slip next purl stitch to cable needle and hold in back. Knit 2, purl the stitch from the cable needle.

Cross front: Slip next 2 stitches to cable needle and hold in front. Purl 1, then knit 2 from cable needle.

Foundation Row: (right side) P3, k2, p1, k2, p3.

Rows 1 & 3: K3, p2, k1, p2, k3.

Row 2: P3, sl next 3 sts to cn and hold in back, k2, sl the p st back to left needle and p it, k2 from cn, p3.

Row 4: P2, Cross back, p1, Cross front, p2.

Row 5: K2, p2, k3, p2, k2.

Row 6: P1, Cross back, p3, Cross front, p1.

Rows 7 & 9: K1, p2, k5, p2, k1.

Row 8: P1, k2, p5, k2, p1.

Row 10: P1, Cross front, p3, Cross back, p1.

Row 11: K2, p2, k3, p2, k2.

Row 12: P2, Cross front, p1, Cross back, p2.

Repeat Rows 1–12 for pattern. (Do not repeat Foundation Row.)

FINISHING: Arrange side panels on each side of center panel so that garter st edges are to the outside. Place panels with right sides facing and sew with yarn and large-eyed needle by catching only the outside lp of each st on each panel.

Fringe: Knot 4 18-inch strands of yarn into every 4th st across each end of afghan.

Fisherman

Shown on page 35

SIZE: approximately 52 × 72 inches including fringe.

MATERIALS: worsted-weight yarn (230 yards per skein): 24 skeins. Knitting needles size 15 or size required to achieve recommended gauge. Size J crochet hook. Bulky cable needle.

GAUGE: 3 sts = 1 inch in stockinette stitch using double strands of yarn.

Be sure to check your gauge before starting. Use any size needles that will give the correct stitch gauge. If your gauge is not correct or if you make adjustments in the size of the afghan, the yarn amounts may not be sufficient.

Special Note: The entire afghan is worked with 2 strands of yarn held together and worked as one. Each of the 3 cable panels measures approximately 14 inches in width. Each of the 2 popcorn panels measures approximately 4½ inches in width. The afghan is worked in panels, then sewn together to finish.

CABLE PANEL: (make 3) Using double strands of yarn, cast on 42 sts.
Row 1: (right side) K5, p5, k2tog, k3, yo, p2, k8, p2, yo, k3, sl 1, k1, psso, p5, k5.
Row 2: K10, p5, k2, p8, k2, p5, k10.
Row 3: K5, p4, k2tog, k3, yo, k1, p2, k8, p2, k1, yo, k3, sl 1, k1, psso, p4, k5.
Row 4: K9, p6, k2, p8, k2, p6, k9.
Row 5: K5, p3, k2tog, k3, yo, k2, p2, k8, p2, k2, yo, k3, sl 1, k1, psso, p3, k5.
Row 6: K8, p7, k2, p8, k2, p7, k8.

Row 7: K5, p2, k2tog, k3, yo, k3, p2, k8, p2, k3, yo, k3, sl 1, k1, psso, p2, k5.
Row 8: K7, p8, k2, p8, k2, p8, k7.
Row 9: K5, p1, k2tog, k3, yo, k4, p2, sl next 4 sts onto cn and hold in back of work, k4, then k the 4 sts from cn, p2, k4, yo, k3, sl 1, k1, psso, p1, k5.
Row 10: K6, p9, k2, p8, k2, p9, k6.
Repeat Rows 1–10 for pattern. Work in pattern until you have 28 cable crosses. Then repeat Rows 1–8. Bind off.

POPCORN PANEL: (make 2) Using double strands of yarn, cast on 15 sts.
Row 1: K1, * (k1, p1, k1) all in next st, p3tog. Repeat from * across to last 2 sts, (k1, p1, k1) in next st, k1 in last st—17 sts.
Row 2: P across row.
Row 3: K1, * p3tog, (k1, p1, k1) all in next st. Repeat from * across to last st, k1—15 sts.
Row 4: P across row.
Repeat Rows 1–4 for pattern. Work in pattern until panel measures same as cable panel.

FINISHING: Sew panels together, alternating a cable panel, popcorn panel, cable panel. Using double strands of yarn, with right side of work facing you, work 1 row of half double crochet across *each end.*

Fringe: Cut strands of yarn 15 inches in length. Each tassel is composed of 6 strands that are folded in half. From the wrong side, insert crochet hook in stitch and pull folded loop through, then bring ends through the loop. Tighten. Attach fringe every 2 inches across each end.

Pretty Petals

Shown on page 36

This afghan comes in two sizes, one for baby and one for adults, as pictured. Adult directions follow the baby afghan directions.

BABY AFGHAN

SIZE: approximately 33 × 44 inches before fringe.

MATERIALS: worsted-weight yarn (240 yards per skeins): 5 skeins. Knitting needles size 8 or size required to achieve recommended gauge.

GAUGE: 1 small square = 5 × 5 inches

Be sure to check your gauge before starting. Use any size needles that will give the correct stitch gauge. If your gauge is not correct or if you make adjustments in the size of the afghan, the yarn amounts may not be sufficient.

Note: To form flower, make four 5-×-5-inch squares. Sew together to form 1 large 10-×-10-inch square, which is steamed to measure 11-×-11-inches. For ease in finishing, when 4 small squares are completed, sew together to form 1 large square.

SMALL SQUARE: (make 48) Cast on 3 sts.

Row 1: Knit.

Note: To increase, knit in front and back of stitch.

Row 2: (right side) Inc one st in first st, k1, inc in last st — 5 sts.
Row 3: K1, p3, k1.
Row 4: Inc in first st, k1, yo, k1, yo, k1, inc one st —9 sts.
Row 5: K2, p5, k2.
Row 6: Inc 1, k3, yo, k1, yo, k3, inc 1—13 sts.

Row 7: K3, p7, k3.
Row 8: Inc 1, k5, yo, k1, yo, k5, inc 1 st—17 sts.
Row 9: K4, p9, k4.
Row 10: Inc 1, k7, yo, k1, yo, k7, inc 1—21 sts.
Row 11: K5, p11, k5.
Row 12: Inc 1, k4, k2tog, k7, sl 1, k1, psso, k4, inc 1 — 21 sts.
Row 13: K6, p9, k6.
Row 14: Inc 1, k5, k2tog, k5, sl 1, k1, psso, k5, inc 1—21 sts.
Row 15: K7, p7, k7.
Row 16: Inc 1, k6, k2tog, k3, sl 1, k1, psso, k6, inc 1 — 21 sts.
Row 17: K8, p5, k8.
Row 18: Inc 1, k7, k2tog, k1, sl 1, k1, psso, k7, inc 1 — 21 sts.
Row 19: K9, p3, k9.
Row 20: Inc 1 st, k8, k3tog, k8, inc 1—21 sts.
Row 21: Purl.
Row 22: K1, * yo, k2tog; repeat from * to end—21 sts.
Row 23: Purl.
Row 24: Inc 1, k to last st, inc 1—23 sts.
Row 25: Knit.
Row 26: Inc 1, p to last st, inc 1—25 sts.
Row 27: Knit.
Row 28: K2tog, k to last 2 sts, k2tog—23 sts.
Row 29: Purl.
Row 30: K1, * k2tog, yo; repeat from * to last 4 sts, (k2tog) twice—21 sts.
Row 31: Purl.
Row 32: Repeat Row 28—19 sts.
Row 33: Knit.
Row 34: P across, p2tog at beg and end—17 sts.
Row 35: Knit.
Row 36: Repeat Row 28—15 sts.
Row 37: Purl.
Rows 38–45: Repeat Rows 30–37—7 sts at end of Row 45.
Row 46: (K2tog) twice, yo, k2tog, k1—5 sts.
Row 47: Purl.
Row 48: K2tog, k1, k2tog—3 sts. K3tog. Fasten off.

LARGE SQUARE: Sew 4 small squares together to make a large square, arranging so that all 4 petals meet in center to form a 4-petal flower. Sew with care to match rows, working from outer rim to center and sewing through "bump" of garter stitches. To draw in center of flower, when last square is sewn, run needle through center stitch of each petal and fasten on wrong side. From wrong side, pin each square out to 11 × 11 inches and steam lightly over damp, not wet, cloth. Allow to dry thoroughly.

FINISHING: Sew large squares together, having 3 across and 4 down.

Fringe: Knot 3 9-inch strands folded in half across upper and lower edge. Trim fringe evenly.

FULL-SIZE AFGHAN

SIZE: approximately 44 × 66 inches before fringe.

Work exactly the same as baby afghan. You will need 10 skeins of worsted-weight yarn (240 yards per skein). Make 96 small squares. Sew 4 squares together as you complete them to form 24 large squares. Sew large squares together with 4 across and 6 down.

Fringe: Knot 3 12-inch strands folded in half across upper and lower edges.

Lullaby Baby Afghan

Directions are given for a baby afghan and a full-size afghan. The adult size directions are given after the baby afghan.

SIZE: approximately 40 × 42 inches.

MATERIALS: sport-weight yarn (220 yards per skein): 6 skeins MC (white) and 2 skeins CC (yellow). Crochet hook size D or size required to achieve recommended gauge.

GAUGE: 1 square = 3½ inches

Be sure to check your gauge before starting. Use any size hook that will give the correct stitch gauge. If your gauge is not correct or if you make adjustments in the size of the afghan, the yarn amounts may not be sufficient.

SQUARE WITH YELLOW FLOWER: (make 66) With MC, ch 4, sl st to join into a circle.

Rnd 1: Ch 1, work 8 sc in circle, sl st to join. Draw CC through lp on hook, break MC, fasten off.
Rnd 2: Pull lp up to measure about ¾ inch, (yo and draw up ¾-inch lp in same place as joining) 4 times, yo then draw yarn through 9 lps on hook, ch 3, * in next sc (yo and draw up ¾-inch lp) 4 times, yo and through the 9 lps on hook, ch 3; repeat from * 6 times. Join with sl st to top of first cluster. Fasten off.
Rnd 3: Attach MC in any ch-3 lp. Ch 2, dc 4 times in same lp, * dc 4 times in next lp, dc 5 times in next lp; repeat

from * around, ending dc 4 times in last lp, join with sl st to top of beg ch-2.
Rnd 4: Ch 2, dc in next st, * (2 dc, ch 1, 2 dc) in next st, dc in next 8 sts; repeat from * ending dc in last 6 sts, sl st to join.
Last Rnd: Work sc around, having 3 sc in each of the 4 corner sts. Fasten off.

SQUARE WITH WHITE FLOWER: (make 66) Work through Rnd 1 with CC. Complete square with MC.

FINISHING: There will be 11 squares across and 12 down. Make 6 strips beg with yellow flower; 5 strips beg with white flower. Alternate strips so that flowers are staggered as shown. To sew squares, place them with right sides facing. With yarn in large-eyed needle, catch only the outside lp of each st of each side of each square, matching corners. With MC, work 1 row hdc around entire afghan, having 3 sts in each corner.

Trim: With MC, * ch 2, sc in 3rd st from hook, sk 2 sts, sc in next st; repeat from * around. Fasten off.

FULL-SIZE LULLABY AFGHAN

SIZE: approximately 55 × 60 inches.

MATERIALS: worsted-weight yarn (220 yards per skein): 12 skeins MC and 4 skeins CC. Crochet hook size H.

Work same as baby afghan using larger hook and worsted-weight yarn.

Indian Blanket

Shown on page 38

SIZE: approximately 56 × 64 inches before fringe.

MATERIALS: worsted-weight yarn (220 yarns per skein): 4 skeins color A (ecru), 3 skeins color B (brick), 5 skeins color C (cranberry), 3 skeins color D (gray). Knitting needles size 8 or size required to achieve recommended gauge. Crochet hook size F; 6 yarn bobbins.

GAUGE: 5 sts = 1 inch
6 rows = 1 inch

Be sure to check your gauge before starting. Use any size needles that will give the correct stitch gauge. If your gauge is not correct or if you make adjustments in the size of the afghan, the yarn amounts may not be sufficient.

AFGHAN

Note: Afghan is worked in panels knit in stockinette stitch. Charts show color placement. Always twist yarns when changing colors to prevent holes. Keep tension even. When the panel is knit, half double crochet and single crochet are worked on each side.

Main Panel: (make 2) With C, cast on 44 sts. Following Chart 1, repeat the 34 rows 10 times. With C, bind off. With D, work 1 row single crochet lengthwise along side of panel (having 22 sts to each repeat of pattern); then work 1 row half double crochet. With B, work 1 row single crochet. Fasten off. *Note:* Always begin single crochet row on right side of work. Work other side of panel the same.

Panel 2: (make 3) With A, cast on 21 sts. Following Chart 2, work the 34 rows 10 times. Bind off. Work crochet along lengthwise edges as for main panel.

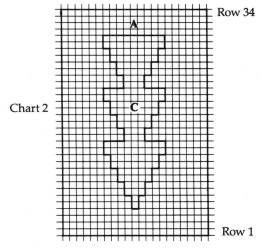

Chart 2

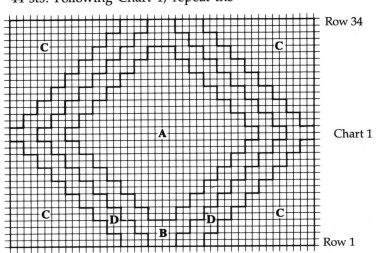

Chart 1

Panel 3: (make 2) With C, cast on 22 sts. Following Chart 3, work the 34 rows 10 times. With C, bind off. With right side facing you, work crochet as for other panels on left side of one panel and right side of other panel. On the other side of each of these panels work 1 row single crochet, then 1 row half double crochet using D only. Fasten off.

Panel 4: (make 2) With B, cast on 10 sts. Repeat the 12 rows of Chart 4 until piece measures same as other panels. Fasten off. On each side of panels work 1 row single crochet, then 1 row half double crochet using D only. Fasten off.

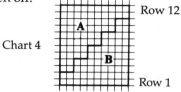

Chart 4

Row 12

Row 1

FINISHING: See chart for placement. Notice where the gray edge on each Panel 3 is placed. To sew panels together: Place right sides together, having bottom edges even. With yarn in large-eyed needle, pick up only the outside loop of stitches from each side. This makes an attractive, flat seam on right side.

Fringe: With C, knot 4 10-inch strands in every 3rd stitch along each end. Trim evenly.

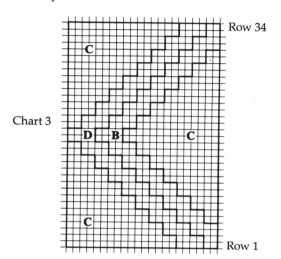

Chart 3

Row 34

Row 1

| Panel 4 (10 sts) |
| Panel 3 (22 sts) *Gray edge* |
| Panel 2 (21 sts) |
| Main Panel (44 sts) |
| Panel 2 (21 sts) |
| Main Panel (44 sts) |
| Panel 2 (21 sts) |
| Panel 3 (22 sts) *Gray edge* |
| Panel 4 (10 sts) |

Traditional Ripple

Shown on page 39

SIZE: approximately 49 × 62 inches, excluding fringe.

MATERIALS: worsted-weight yarn (240 yards per skein): 4 skeins color A (off-white), 3 skeins color B (peach), 3 skeins color C (coral) and 3 skeins color D (salmon). Crochet hook size I or size required to achieve recommended gauge.

GAUGE: 19 sts (1 pattern repeat) = 4 inches measured from point to point; 24 rows (1 color repeat) = 10 inches measured straight up side.

Be sure to check your gauge before starting. Use any size hook that will give the correct stitch gauge. If your gauge is not correct or if you make adjustments in the size of the afghan, the yarn amounts may not be sufficient.

AFGHAN: With A, ch 246.

Row 1: Sc in 2nd ch from hook, sc in each of next 7 ch, * 3 sc in next ch, 1 sc in each of next 8 ch, skip 2 ch, 1 sc in each of next 8 ch; repeat from * 11 times more, end 3 sc in next ch, 1 sc in each of last 8 ch. Ch 1, turn.

Note: Ch 1, turn at end of each row. Work in back lp of all sc.

Row 2: Working in back lp of each sc across, sk first sc, * 1 sc in each of next 8 sc, 3 sc in next sc, 1 sc in each of next 8 sc, sk 2 sc; repeat from *, end 1 sc in each of next 8 sc, 3 sc in next sc, 1 sc in each of next 8 sc. Do not work end st. Repeat Row 2 for pattern working as follows: 2 more rows A, * 2 rows B, 4 rows C, 2 rows D, 2 rows A, 4 rows B, 2 rows C, 4 rows D, 4 rows A *. Repeat the 24 rows between *'s 5 times more—6 color repeats plus 4 more rows A. Fasten off.

Fringe: Cut 14-inch strands of all 4 colors. Use 4 strands of A on each point. Alternate fringe of B, C and D on indented points, using 4 strands for each fringe. Fold 4 strands in half and knot fringe.

Do not block.

Quick Popcorn

Shown on page 40

SIZE: approximately 40 × 62 inches.

MATERIALS: bulky-weight brushed acrylic yarn (80 yards per skein): 13 skeins. Size Q crochet hook or size required to achieve recommended gauge.

GAUGE: 6 dc = 4 inches
3 rows = 3½ inches

Be sure to check your gauge before starting. Use any size hook that will give the correct stitch gauge. If your gauge is not correct, or if you make adjustments in the size of the afghan, the yarn amounts may not be sufficient.

Note: This afghan is worked in 1 piece. The turning chain always counts as one double crochet.

AFGHAN: Ch 51 loosely.

Row 1: Work 1 dc in 4th ch from hook and in each ch across—49 dc. Ch 2, turn.
Rows 2 & 3: (dc row) Work 1 dc in 2nd st from hook and in each st across row, working the last dc into the turning ch of previous row—49 dc. Ch 2, turn.
Row 4: (popcorn row; right side of work) Work 1 dc in 2nd st from hook. Dc in next dc. * Ch 1, 4 dc all in next st, drop lp off hook. Insert hook from front to back in the ch-1. Pick up dropped lp with hook and draw lp through ch-1 tightly (popcorn complete). Work 1 dc in each of next 5 sts. Repeat from * across, ending with popcorn and 3 dc. (Last dc is worked in turning ch of previous row.)
Rows 5, 6 and 7: Repeat Row 2—49 sts.
Row 8: Work 1 dc in 2nd st from hook and in each of next 4 sts, * popcorn in next st, 1 dc in each of next 5 sts. Repeat from * across, ending with popcorn and 6 dc. Work in following pattern: Work dc row (Row 2) 3 times, work Row 4. Work dc row 3 times; then work Row 8. Repeat these rows until afghan measures correct length (approximately 13 popcorn rows), ending with 3 dc rows.

Edging: Starting at any corner, with right side of work facing you, attach yarn. Being careful to keep afghan flat, work 1 row hdc around entire afghan, working 2 hdc in each corner.

Ruffle Rnd: Ch 4, work 3 tr in same st. * Ch 1, sk 1 st, 4 tr all in next st. Repeat from * around afghan, ending with sl st to join in beg ch-4. Fasten off. Weave in loose ends.

Quick and Easy Diamonds

Shown on page 41

SIZE: approximately 48 × 54 inches, excluding fringe.

MATERIALS: worsted-weight yarn (230 yards per skein): 15 skeins. Knitting needles size 35 or size required to achieve recommended gauge.

GAUGE: 1½ sts = 1 inch in stockinette stitch, using 4 strands of yarn held together and worked as one

Be sure to check your gauge before starting. Use any size needles that will give the correct stitch gauge. If your gauge is not correct, or if you make adjustments in the size of the afghan, the yarn amounts may not be sufficient.

Special Note: 15 skeins of yarn will make this afghan. One of these skeins will be used to make the tassels for the corners. This leaves 14 remaining skeins with which to complete the afghan. The pattern calls for you to work 4 strands of yarn together. Using the 14 skeins of yarn, you have 3 sets of 4 skeins (12 total skeins) with 2 skeins left over. Divide each of these 2 remaining skeins in half and you will then have 4 strands to work together.

AFGHAN

Holding 4 strands of yarn tog, cast on 73 sts. (Your needle will be a bit crowded. Push the sts tog tightly and they will all fit.)

Row 1: K1, * p1, k9, p1, k1. Repeat from * across row.
Row 2: K1, * p1, k1, p7, k1, p1, k1. Repeat from * across row.
Row 3: K1, * p1, k1, p1, k5, p1, k1, p1, k1. Repeat from * across row.
Row 4: P1, * p1, k1, p1, k1, p3, k1, p1, k1, p2. Repeat from * across row.
Row 5: K1, * k2, p1, k1, p1, k1, p1, k1, p1, k3. Repeat from * across row.
Row 6: P1, * p3, k1, p1, k1, p1, k1, p4. Repeat from * across row.
Row 7: K1, * k4, p1, k1, p1, k5. Repeat from * across row.
Row 8: Repeat Row 6.
Row 9: Repeat Row 5.
Row 10: Repeat Row 4.
Row 11: Repeat Row 3.
Row 12: Repeat Row 2.
Repeat Rows 1–12 of the pattern st 8 times more—108 rows total.

FINISHING: Bind off loosely. Make 4 tassels, one for each corner. Cut a piece of cardboard 6 inches wide. Wind yarn around the cardboard approximately 50 times. Slip the yarn off and, holding the loop firmly, thread a needle with the yarn and take it through the top of the loop twice and secure. Break yarn. Wind the same yarn around the tassel several times about ½ inch from top and secure. Cut through bottom of loop to form tassel. Sew tassels onto afghan corners. Weave in loose ends.

Delightful Pennsylvania Dutch

Shown on page 42

SIZE: approximately 52 × 78 inches.

MATERIALS: worsted-weight yarn: 48 ounces MC (white), 34 ounces color A (red), 6 ounces color B (blue), 3½ ounces color C (green), 1 ounce each of color D (black) and color E (yellow). Crochet hook size F or size required to achieve correct gauge.

GAUGE: Each motif measures 6½ inches square.

Be sure to check your gauge before starting. Use any size hook that will give the correct stitch gauge. If your gauge is not correct or if you make adjustments in the size of the afghan, the yarn amounts may not be sufficient.

Note: Flower is worked first and then attached on Row 1 of the motif.

FLOWER: *Rnd 1:* 8 sc in 2nd ch from hook. Join and fasten off.
Rnd 2: Attach B to first sc and, working loosely, * ch 4, holding back on hook the last lp of each tr, make 2 tr in same sc, yo and draw through all lps on hook, ch 4, sl st in same sc, sl st in next sc. Repeat from * around. Join and fasten off—8 petals.

MOTIF: With A, ch 6. Join with sl st to form ring.
Rnd 1: Sl st in ring, ch 5, with wrong side of flower facing you, sl st in tip of any petal, ch 5, sl st in ring, * ch 5, sl st in tip of next petal, ch 5, sl st in ring. Repeat from * around. Join and fasten off.
Rnd 2: With right side of flower facing you, attach A to ch-5 lp following sl st at tip of any petal, sc in same place, * ch 3, sc in next ch-5 lp preceding sl st of next petal, sc in lp following sl st. Repeat from * around, ending with sc in last free ch-5 lp. Join.
Rnd 3: Sl st in next sp, ch 3, in same sp make 2 dc, ch 3 and 3 dc; * make 3 dc in next sp, in next sp make 3 dc, ch 3 and 3 dc. Repeat from * around. Join to top of ch-3. Fasten off.
Rnd 4: With right side facing, attach MC to any corner sp, ch 3, in same sp make 2 dc, ch 3 and 3 dc, * dc in each dc to next corner sp, in corner sp make 3 dc, ch 3 and 3 dc. Repeat from * around. Join. There will be 15 dc between corner chains.

Now work in rows as follows:
Row 1: Sl st to center ch of corner, sl st in sp, ch 3, dc in each dc to next corner sp, in corner sp make 2 dc, ch 3 and 2 dc; dc in each dc to next corner sp, dc in sp. Ch 1, turn.
Row 2: Sc in each dc to next sp, 3 sc in sp, sc in each dc across, sc in top of ch-3. Ch 3, turn.
Row 3: Skip first sc, dc in next sc and in each sc to center sc of corner, in corner sc make 2 dc, ch 3 and 2 dc; dc in each remaining sc. Ch 1, turn.
Rows 4 & 5: Repeat Rows 2 & 3.

Now work around motif as follows:
Rnd 1: Ch 1, turn and sc around all 4 sides, working 3 sc in corners, and 23 sc on each side. Join and break off.
Rnd 2: Attach A to center sc at any corner, 3 sc in same place, sc in each sc around, making 3 sc in center sc at each corner. Join and break off.

Embroidery: With single strand of C, embroider 2 stems in chain st. With 2 strands of C, embroider 2 leaves in lazy daisy st. With E, fasten center of flower to motif by making a row of backstitches around D section. Sew motifs neatly together in pattern, making 8 rows of 12 motifs.

Edging: *Rnd 1:* Attach A to any corner, make 3 sc in same place, sc closely around, making 3 sc in each corner. Join.
Rnd 2: Sc in each sc around, making 3 sc in each corner sc.
Join and finish off.
Block to measurements.

SIZE: approximately 44 × 66 inches, excluding fringe.

MATERIALS: worsted-weight yarn (205 yards; 3.5-ounce skeins): 10 skeins color A (navy), 4 skeins color B (white), 2 skeins each of color C (red) and color D (green). Knitting needles size 9 or size required for gauge; size G crochet hook.

GAUGE: 4 sts = 1 inch
6 rows = 1 inch

Be sure to check your gauge before starting. Use any size needles that will give the correct stitch gauge. If your gauge is not correct, or if you make adjustments in the size of the afghan, the yarn amounts may not be sufficient.

Note: Vertical stripes will be crocheted after knitting has been completed.

Starting at a narrow edge with A, cast on 164 sts.
Rows 1–6: With A, work in St st (k 1 row, p 1 row) for 6 rows. Drop A; attach B.
Row 7: With B, k across. Drop B; attach C.
Rows 8–9: With C, p 1 row, k 1 row. Fasten off C; pick up B.
Row 10: With B, p across. Fasten off B; pick up A.

Note: Always carry A loosely along side edge of work.

Rows 11–24: With A, work in St st for 14 rows. Drop A; attach B.
Rows 25–28: Using D instead of C, repeat Rows 7–10. Fasten off B; pick up A.
Rows 29–42: With A, work in St st for 14 rows. Repeat last 36 rows (Rows 7–42) for pattern. Work in pattern until total length is about 66 inches, end with 6 rows A.

Next Row: With A, bind off first 9 sts, * drop next st off left-hand needle, pull out st on right-hand needle to measure about ½ inch, bind off 10 sts. Repeat from * across. Unravel each dropped st all the way down to cast-on edge. With A and a darning needle, secure st to cast-on edge. Ridges formed by dropped sts will be used to work vertical stripes.

VERTICAL STRIPES: With right side facing, starting at cast-on edge, with crochet hook attach B to base of first ridge formed by dropped st, holding yarn in back of work, sl st over loose strand of next row, sl st over loose strand of each row across to top edge, sl st over st above at top edge. Fasten off.
Row 2: Attach C to base of same ridge at lower edge, directly next to last row of sl sts; placing sts right next to previous row, work same as for Row 1. Fasten off.
Row 3: With B, repeat Row 2. This completes first stripe. Alternating D and C for center row of stripes, always using B for Rows 1 and 3, work stripes along each ridge throughout afghan.

EDGING: With right side facing, using crochet hook and A, attach yarn to any corner st, ch 1, make 3 sc in same st where yarn was attached; being careful to keep work flat, sc evenly along entire outer edge, making 3 sc in same st at each corner. Join with sl st to first sc. Fasten off.
Pin to measurements on a padded surface; cover with a damp cloth and allow to dry; do not press.

FRINGE: Matching colors of afghan and stripes, work fringe around outer edge. Cut 12-inch strands. Fold strand in half to form loop. Insert hook from back to front and draw loop through. Draw loose ends through loop on hook; pull tight. Trim fringe evenly.

Honeycomb

Shown on page 44

SIZE: approximately 45 × 64 inches.

MATERIALS: worsted-weight yarn (230 yards per skein): 9 skeins dark color (blue) and 7 skeins light color (white). Knitting needles size 15 or size required to achieve recommended gauge; crochet hook size H.

GAUGE: 20 sts = 9 inches; 1 block measures 8 × 9 inches

Be sure to check your gauge before starting. Use any size needle that will give the correct stitch gauge. If your gauge is not correct or if you make adjustments in the size of the afghan, the yarn amounts may not be sufficient.

SPECIAL ABBREVIATIONS:
L......2 strands of light yarn
D......2 strands of dark yarn
LD.....1 strand of light yarn and 1 strand of dark yarn

HONEYCOMB STITCH:
Row 1: (wrong side) Knit.
Row 2: * Knit 1, knit in row below (insert needle in center of stitch below the stitch on the needle, bring yarn through, let stitch above slip off needle). Repeat from * across.
Row 3: Knit.
Row 4: * Knit in row below, knit 1. Repeat from * across.
Repeat Rows 1–4, changing colors as indicated.

GENERAL INSTRUCTIONS: Blocks are knit in a continuous strip. There will be 5 strips. Diagrams show the color placement. The 3 shades shown in the diagram are worked with only 2 colors. The entire afghan is worked with 2 strands of yarn. The light shade is 2 strands of light yarn; the medium shade is 1 strand of light and 1 strand of dark; the dark shade is 2 strands of dark.
Each block begins with 2 rows of the

first color of the block. Color changes begin on the 3rd row. All color changes will be on either Row 1 or Row 3 (wrong-side rows). The 2nd color begins on the 3rd row of the block and always starts with just 1 stitch. Increase the 2nd color on every wrong-side row. As the 2nd color increases, the first color decreases, thus forming the diagonal.

SQUARE

Diagonals from lower right to upper left:
2nd color begins at *end* of wrong-side row.

Diagonals from lower left to upper right:
2nd color begins at beginning of wrong-side row.

When changing colors, always drop 1 color on wrong side and move new color to knit position. Twist new color around old color to prevent a hole. Continue increasing 1 stitch of 2nd color each wrong-side row until you are working with only the 2nd color. Work 2 rows with 2nd color. Rows 2 and 4 (right-side rows) are always worked in colors used on Rows 1 and 3.

STRIPS 1, 3 & 5:

Note: Each block begins with a wrong-side row and ends with a right-side row. Do not fasten off at end of block.

First block: With D, cast on 20 sts. Working in Honeycomb Stitch, work 2 rows with D only. Beg LD at beg of next row. Continue to inc 1 st of LD each wrong-side row until all sts on needle are LD. Work 2 rows LD ending after Row 2 of Honeycomb Stitch.

2nd block: Beg with Row 3, work 2 rows with L. At end of next row, beg LD. Inc LD each wrong-side row until entire row is LD. Work 2 rows of LD.

3rd block: Work 42 rows in pattern with D only.

4th block: Work first 2 rows with LD. Beg L at beg of next row. Continue to inc L until entire row is L. Work 2 rows of L.

5th block: Work first 2 rows with D. Start LD at end of next row. Inc LD each wrong-side row until entire row is LD. Work 2 rows LD.

6th block: Work 42 rows with D only.

7th block: Work first 2 rows with LD. Beg L at beg of next row. Continue to inc L until entire row is L. Work 2 rows of L.

8th block: Work first 2 rows with LD. Beg D at end of next row. Continue to inc D until entire row is D. Work 2 rows of D. Bind off.

STRIPS 2 & 4:

First block: With D, cast on 20 sts. Working in Honeycomb Stitch, work 2 rows with D only. Work last st of next row with LD. Continue to inc LD each wrong-side row until entire row is LD. Work 2 rows LD, ending after Row 2.

2nd block: Work 2 rows with L. Work first st with LD at beg of next row; continue row with L. Inc LD on each wrong-side row. Work last 2 rows with LD.

3rd block: Work 42 rows with L.

4th block: Work 2 rows with LD. Start D at end of next row. Inc D on each wrong-side row. Work last 2 rows with D.

5th block: Work 2 rows with L. Work first st with LD at beg of next row. Inc LD on each wrong-side row. Work last 2 rows with LD.

6th block: Work 42 rows with L.

7th block: Work 2 rows LD. Beg L at end of next row. Continue to inc L. Work last 2 rows L.

8th block: Work 2 rows LD. Beg D at beg of next row. Continue to inc D. Work last 2 rows D. Bind off.

FINISHING: Block all strips. Sew strips together, following diagram. With LD and right side of work facing you, single crochet evenly along long side edges.

Tassels: (make 4) Wind dark yarn around a 5½-inch piece of cardboard approximately 40–50 times. Cut 2 15-inch strands of yarn. Slip 1 strand under yarn at top edge. Tie tightly and slip tassel off cardboard. Tie 2nd strand of yarn tightly approximately 1 inch from top. Cut loose ends at bottom. Trim evenly. Attach 1 tassel to each corner.

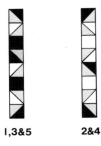

1,3&5   2&4

KEY

■ Dark
▨ Light & Dark
□ Light

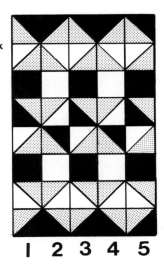

1 2 3 4 5

Mad for Plaid

Shown on page 45

SIZE: approximately 50 × 54 inches, excluding fringe.

MATERIALS: worsted-weight yarn (230 yards per skein): 6 skeins color A (dark), 5 skeins color B (light) and 2 skeins color C (off-white). Size G crochet hook or size required to achieve recommended gauge. Large-eyed yarn needle.

GAUGE: 2 rows = 1 inch
Dc, ch 1, dc, ch 1 = 1 inch

Be sure to check your gauge before starting. Use any size hook that will give the correct stitch gauge. If your gauge is not correct or if you make adjustments in the size of the afghan, the yarn amounts may not be sufficient.

AFGHAN: With A, ch 191.

Row 1: Dc in 5th ch from hook, * ch 1, sk 1, dc in next ch, repeat from * across—94 sp. Ch 4, turn. Ch 4 counts as first dc and ch 1 of next row.
Row 2: Dc in next dc, * ch 1, dc in next dc, repeat from * across, ending with dc in 3rd ch of turning ch. Ch 4, turn.

Repeating Row 2, work 4 more rows with A. Continue in following sequence starting with the 4 rows of B.

Color sequence for rows: * 6 rows A, 4 rows B, 2 rows C, 2 rows A, 2 rows B, 2 rows A, 2 rows C, 4 rows B, repeat from * 4 more times. Work 6 rows A—126 rows.

Vertical weaving: Wind each color of yarn into 3 balls. Using large-eyed yarn needle threaded with 3 strands of same color, weave yarn vertically through spaces. Begin at side edge, weave *over* and *under* each mesh space, leaving 7 inches for fringe at each end. Cut yarn. Weave 2nd vertical row beginning with *under*, then *over*. Continue to alternate weaving each row in the following sequence: * 4 rows A, 2 rows B, 2 rows C, 2 rows A, 2 rows B, 2 rows A, 2 rows C, 2 rows B. Repeat from * 4 more times, ending with 4 rows A.

Work 1 row sc along edges with A.

Fringe: Knot 3 strands of one row with 3 strands of next row. Repeat along both ends. Trim evenly.

X-Cellent Choice for a Sailor

Shown on page 46

SIZE: approximately 50 × 71 inches.

MATERIALS: worsted-weight yarn (3.5-ounce skein, 230 yards per skein): 17 skeins. Crochet hook sizes H and J or size required to achieve recommended gauge.

GAUGE: 3 dc = 1 inch using smaller hook; 3 rows = 2 inches

Be sure to check your gauge before starting. Use any size hook that will give the correct stitch gauge. If your gauge is not correct or if you make adjustments in the size of the afghan, the yarn amounts may not be sufficient.

PATTERN STITCHES WITH ABBREVIATIONS:

Popcorn (PC): On right side of work, 4 double crochet in next double crochet, drop loop from hook, insert

hook from *front* to *back* in first double crochet of 4-double crochet group and draw dropped loop through (Fig. 1), chain 1.

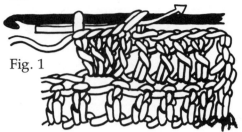

Fig. 1

Back Popcorn (BPC): On wrong side, work 4 double crochet in next double crochet, drop loop from hook, insert hook from *back* to *front* in first double crochet of 4-double crochet group and draw dropped loop through, chain 1.

Front Post Double Crochet (FPdc): On right side of work and with yarn in front, you will work around post of double crochet of previous row. Yarn

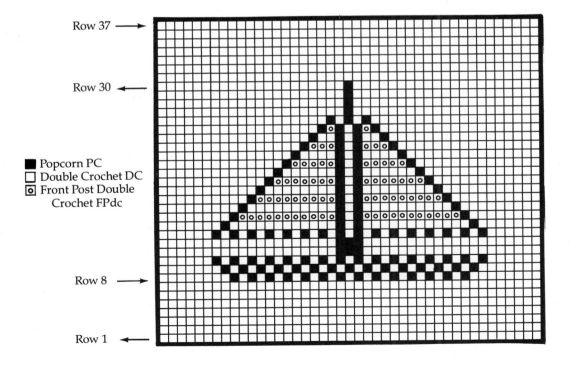

■ Popcorn PC
□ Double Crochet DC
◉ Front Post Double
　Crochet FPdc

69

over, insert hook from *front* to *back* and around to *front* again, yarn over, and draw up a 1/2-inch loop (Fig. 2), (yarn over and draw through 2 loops) twice. Always skip the double crochet behind the FPdc.

Fig. 2

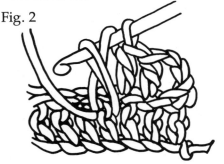

AFGHAN: (Make 3 panels) Turning ch always counts as first dc.

Row 1: (Row 1 of Design Chart) On right side, with smaller hook, ch 45 loosely, dc in 4th st from hook, * dc in next st; repeat from * across—43 dc. Ch 3, turn.

Rows 2–7: Dc in each st across—43 dc counting beg ch-3 as 1 dc. Ch 3, turn.

Row 8: Dc in each of next 7 dc, * work BPC in next dc, dc in next st; repeat from * 13 times more, dc in each of the next 8 sts. Ch 3, turn.

Row 9: Dc in each of next 6 dc, * work PC in next st, dc in next st (do not dc in the ch-1 that ends the BPC st of previous row unless otherwise specified); repeat from * 14 times more, dc in each of next 7 sts. Ch 3, turn.

Row 10: Dc in each of next 5 dc, * work BPC in next dc, dc in next st (do not dc in the ch-1 that ends the PC st of previous row unless otherwise specified); repeat from * 15 times more, dc in each of next 6 sts. Ch 3, turn.

Row 11: Dc in each of next 19 sts, PC in ch-1 of BPC st of previous row, Pc in next dc, PC in ch-1 sp of BPC st of previous row, dc in each of next 20 sts. Ch 3, turn.

Row 12: Dc in each of next 19 sts, work BPC in each *ch-1* of next 3 PC sts of previous row, dc in each of next 20 sts. Ch 3, turn.

Row 13: Dc in each of next 5 dc, * PC in next st, dc in next st; repeat from * 6 times, PC in *ch-1 sp* of BPC of previous

row, dc in *ch-1 sp* of center BPC of previous row, PC in *ch-1 sp* of BPC of previous row, dc in next dc; ** PC in next st, dc in next st; repeat from ** 6 times, dc in each of next 6 sts. Ch 3, turn.

Row 14: Dc in each of next 6 sts, work BPC in next st, dc in each of next 12 sts, BPC in *ch-1 sp* of PC of previous row, dc in next dc, BPC in *ch-1 sp* of PC of previous row, dc in each of next 12 sts, BPC in next st, dc in each of next 7 sts. Ch 3, turn.

Row 15: Dc in each of next 7 sts, work PC in next st, FPdc around post of each of next 11 dc, PC in *ch-1 sp* of BPC of previous row, dc in next dc, PC in *ch-1 sp* of BPC of previous row, FPdc around post of next 11 dc, PC in next st, dc in each of next 8 sts. Ch 3, turn.

Row 16: Dc in each of next 8 sts, work BPC in next st, dc in each of next 10 sts, BPC in *ch-1 sp* of PC of previous row, dc in next dc, BPC in *ch-1 sp* of PC of previous row, dc in each of next 10 sts, BPC in next st, dc in each of next 9 sts. Ch 3, turn.

Row 17: Dc in each of next 9 sts, work PC in next st, FPdc around post of each of next 9 dc, PC in *ch-1 sp* of BPC of previous row, dc in next dc, PC in *ch-1 sp* of BPC of previous row, FPdc around post of each of next 9 dc, PC in next st, dc in each of next 10 sts. Ch 3, turn.

Row 18: Dc in each of next 10 sts, work BPC in next st, dc in each of next 8 sts, BPC in *ch-1 sp* of PC of previous row, dc in next dc, BPC in *ch-1 sp* of PC of previous row, dc in each of next 8 sts, BPC in next st, dc in each of next 11 sts. Ch 3, turn.

Row 19: Dc in each of next 11 sts, work PC in next st, FPdc around post of each of next 7 dc, PC in *ch-1 sp* of BPC of previous row, dc in next dc, PC in *ch-1 sp* of BPC of previous row, FPdc around post of each of next 7 dc, PC in next st, dc in each of next 12 sts. Ch 3, turn.

Row 20: Dc in each of next 12 sts, work BPC in next st, dc in each of next 6 sts, BPC in *ch-1 sp* of previous row, dc in next dc, BPC in *ch-1 sp* of PC of previous row, dc in each of next 6 sts, BPC in next st, dc in each of next 13 sts. Ch

3, turn.

Row 21: Dc in each of next 13 sts, work PC in next st, FPdc around post of each of next 5 dc, PC in *ch-1 sp* of BPC of previous row, dc in next dc, PC in *ch-1 sp* of BPC of previous row, FPdc around post of each of next 5 dc, PC in next st, dc in each of next 14 sts. Ch 3, turn.

Row 22: Dc in each of next 14 sts, work BPC in next st, dc in each of next 4 dc, BPC in *ch-1 sp* of PC of previous row, dc in next dc, BPC in *ch-1 sp* of PC of previous row, dc in each of next 4 sts, BPC in next st, dc in each of next 15 sts. Ch 3, turn.

Row 23: Dc in each of next 15 sts, work PC in next st, FPdc around post of each of next 3 dc, PC in *ch-1 sp* of BPC of previous row, dc in next dc, PC in *ch-1 sp* of BPC of previous row, FPdc around post of each of next 3 dc, PC in next st, dc in each of next 16 sts. Ch 3, turn.

Row 24: Dc in each of next 16 sts, work BPC in next st, dc in each of next 2 dc, BPC in *ch-1 sp* of PC of previous row, dc in next dc, BPC in *ch-1 sp* of PC of previous row, dc in each of next 2 sts, BPC in next st, dc in each of next 17 sts. Ch 3, turn.

Row 25: Dc in each of next 17 sts, work PC in next st, FPdc around post of next dc, PC in *ch-1 sp* of BPC of previous row, dc in next dc, PC in *ch-1 sp* of BPC of previous row, FPdc around post of next dc, PC in next st, dc in each of next 18 sts. Ch 3, turn.

Row 26: Dc in each of next 18 sts, work BPC in FPdc of previous row, dc in next PC st, BPC in next dc, dc in next PC st, BPC in next FPdc, dc in each of next 19 sts. Ch 3, turn.

Row 27: Dc in each of next 20 sts, work PC in *ch-1 sp* of BPC of previous row, dc in each of next 21 sts. Ch 3, turn.

Row 28: Dc in each of next 20 sts, work BPC in *ch-1 sp* of PC of previous row, dc in each of next 21 sts. Ch 3, turn.

Row 29: Repeat Row 27.

Row 30: Repeat Row 28.

Rows 31–36: Dc in each st across—43 dc. Ch 3, turn.

Row 37: Dc in each st across. Ch 1, turn.

DO NOT BREAK YARN. Change to larger crochet hook.

Row 38: Sc in each st across—43 sc. Ch 3, turn.

Row 39 CABLE PATTERN STITCH: *Note:* Each cable is completed before the next cable is begun; you will reverse direction twice to complete each separate cable. Row 1: Sc in first st, ch 3, sk 2 sts, sc in next st, turn. Sc in each of the 3 ch (Fig. 3), sl st in the sc before ch was begun (Fig. 4), turn (cable made). Holding the cable toward you, work 1 sc in each of the 2 skipped sts below the cable (Fig. 5).

Fig. 3

Fig. 4

Slip Stitch Here

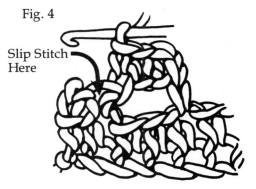

Fig. 5

* Ch 3, sk the sc where the previous ch is attached and the next 2 sts; sc in the next st, turn. Sc in each of the 3 ch, sl st in the sc before ch was begun, turn. Holding cable toward you, sc in the skipped sts as before. Repeat from * across, ending with sc in last st (same sc used to attach last ch-3); ch 1, turn.

Row 40: Work 2 sc in first sc behind first cable, sc in the next sc behind cable (3 sts behind cable), * work 2 sc in first sc behind next cable, sc in next sc. Repeat from * across, ending by working sc in first sc of Row 1.
Row 41: Repeat Row 39.
Row 42: Repeat Row 40.

DO NOT BREAK YARN. Change to smaller crochet hook. Ch 3, turn.

Row 43: Dc in each st across. Ch 3, turn.

Repeat Rows 2–43 one time; repeat Rows 2–37 one time—121 total rows.

DO NOT BREAK YARN.

Panel border:
Rnd 1: With larger crochet hook and wrong side of work facing you, ch 1, 3 sc in corner st, sc in each st across end of panel, work 3 sc in corner st; work 2 sc over each dc st at end of row, work 1 sc in each of the 5 sc in Cable Pattern rows across side of panels; work 3 sc in corner st, work sc in each sc across end of panel, work 3 sc in corner st; work 2 sc over each dc st at end of row, work 1 sc in each of the 5 sc in Cable Pattern rows across side of panel. Join with sl st in beg ch-1. Ch 1, turn.
Rnds 2–3: Follow directions for Rows 39 and 40 of Cable Pattern Stitch. Finish off; weave in ends.

Joining panels: Join panels so all boats are upright. Join with right sides of panels facing you, attach yarn in corner sc of 2 panels. Using larger crochet hook, ch 1, loosely sl st corresponding sts across (working through the front lps of sc) and inserting hook into both sts to make each sl st. Join other panel to these 2 in same manner.

Afghan border:
Rnd 1: With right side facing and using larger crochet hook, attach yarn in *front lp* of sc in lower right-hand corner of afghan. Ch 1, sl st loosely in FRONT LP ONLY of each st around. Join with sl st in beg ch-1. Ch 1, turn.
Rnd 2: Work 3 sc in corner st working in lp of sc not worked in Rnd 1; sc in lp of sc not worked in Rnd 1 of each st across short end of afghan to corner, work 3 sc in corner st; sc in lp of sc not worked in Rnd 1 of each st across side edge of afghan, work 3 sc in corner st; sc in lp of sc not worked in Rnd 1 of each st across side edge of afghan, work 3 sc in corner st; sc in lp of sc not worked in Rnd 1 of each st across short end of afghan. Join with sl st in beg ch-1.
Rnds 3–4: Follow directions for Rows 39 and 40 of Cable Pattern Stitch.
Rnd 5: Ch 1, turn, sl st loosely in FRONT LP ONLY of each st around. Join with sl st in beg ch-1. Ch 1, turn.
Rnd 6: * Sl st in lp of sc not worked in Rnd 5; repeat from * around. Join with sl st in beg ch-1. Fasten off; weave in ends.

Tropical Flowers Afghan & Pillow

Shown on page 47

SIZE: approximately 46 × 57 inches before fringe.

MATERIALS: worsted-weight yarn (220 yards per skein): 12 skeins MC. Needlepoint or crewel yarn for embroidery: 150 yards cardinal, 200 yards rose, 150 yards light geranium, 40 yards pink, 36 yards dark colonial blue, 36 yards navy, 40 yards chestnut, 110 yards dark green, 90 yards medium green and 90 yards light green. Afghan hook size H or size required to achieve recommended gauge. Crochet hook size I.

GAUGE: 9 sts = 2 inches
17 rows = 4 inches

Each panel measures approximately 10 inches wide before crochet border.

Be sure to check your gauge before starting. Use any size hook that will give the correct stitch gauge. If your gauge is not correct or if you make adjustments in the size of the afghan, the yarn amounts may not be sufficient.

AFGHAN

Afghan Stitch Panel: (make 3) Ch loosely 46 sts.

Row 1—First half: Insert hook in top lp only of 2nd ch from hook, draw up lp, * insert hook in top lp of next st, draw up lp; repeat from * across. There will be 46 lps on hook.

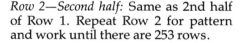

Row 1—Second half: Catch yarn and draw through 1 lp, * catch yarn and draw through 2 lps on hook; repeat from * across until there is only 1 lp on hook. This lp is the beg st of next row.
Row 2—First half: Insert hook under first upright st or vertical bar, catch yarn and draw through, forming lp on hook. Continue drawing up lps in this manner across row.

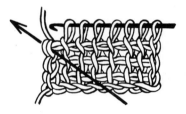

Row 2—Second half: Same as 2nd half of Row 1. Repeat Row 2 for pattern and work until there are 253 rows.

Bind off: Starting on first half of Row 2, sk first bar, * insert hook in next bar, catch yarn and draw loosely through bar and lp on hook; repeat from * across. Break yarn and draw through remaining lp.

Cross stitch embroidery: Chart must of necessity be small in the book. If you find this difficult to see or follow, you can easily transfer the design to ordinary 4-to-the-inch graph paper. There are 46 squares across and 83 up and down. Each square of design represents 1 cross stitch in the color denoted by symbol. The cross stitches are worked in the holes each side of each bar. Do not pull stitches too tight. Work all first stitches of cross slanting

TOP

Ecru 4000

Green Wisp 79

Deep Spruce 112

Dark Green 22

Cardinal 81

Beauty Rose 78

Lt. Geranium 204

Dark Pink 174

Night Shadow 52

Navy Blue 49

Chestnut 265

Each square of this
chart represents
a square of your
afghan panel.

Work from
bottom to top.

to the right and all 2nd stitches of cross slanting to the left for uniformity. The chart is repeated 3 times from bottom to top on each panel, leaving 2 stitches unworked at top and bottom, and 3 stitches on each side of design.

Crochet Borders: When panels have been embroidered and all loose strands worked in, turn panel lengthwise. With MC beg on right side, attach yarn and ch 1, sc in each st down side of panel, working 2 sc in one st near center to make an even number of sts.

Next Row: Ch 3, * sk one st, dc in next st, then dc in st just skipped (forms a crocheted cross st). Repeat from *, ending dc in last st. Repeat this last row 4 more times. Fasten off. Repeat the sc row, then the 5 crocheted cross st rows on each side of each panel.

FINISHING: Place panels with right sides facing and sew tog by catching only the outside lp of each st on each side of each panel. With MC work 1 row sc across top easing in as necessary to lie flat, having an even number of sts. Repeat the crocheted cross st row 1 time. Fasten off. Work bottom the same.

Fringe: With MC, knot 3 14-inch strands of yarn in each crocheted cross st sp across each end. Trim.

AFGHAN STITCH PILLOW

SIZE: approximately 14 inches square.

MATERIALS: worsted-weight yarn (220 yards per skein): 2 skeins MC. Needlepoint or crewel yarn for embroidery: 8 yards cardinal, 16 yards rose, 16 yards light geranium, 16 yards pink, 3 yards dark colonial blue, 3 yards navy, 4 yards chestnut, 8 yards dark green, 16 yards medium green and 8 yards light green. Afghan hook size H or size required to achieve recommended gauge.

GAUGE: 9 sts = 1 inch
4 rows = 1 inch

Note: Pull stitches up to keep 4 rows per inch. You must obtain the given gauge to make your pillow pieces square.

PILLOW PIECES: (make 2) Chain 64 sts with MC and work same as afghan panel until there are 56 rows. Bind off.

Follow the chart for Tropical Flowers pillow, work across stitch embroidery, counting stitches to aid in design placement. Each square of the chart equals 1 square of your pillow top. Back piece is not embroidered.

FINISHING: With MC, work 1 row sc around all 4 sides of pillow pieces. Break yarn and work in threads. Place back and front of pillow together with wrong sides facing each other. Beg at corner about 1/4 inch inside edge, with crochet hook work sl st through both thicknesses around, leaving 1 side open. Insert pillow (purchased or made to fit) or fill with stuffing and continue sl st across the open end. Fasten off.

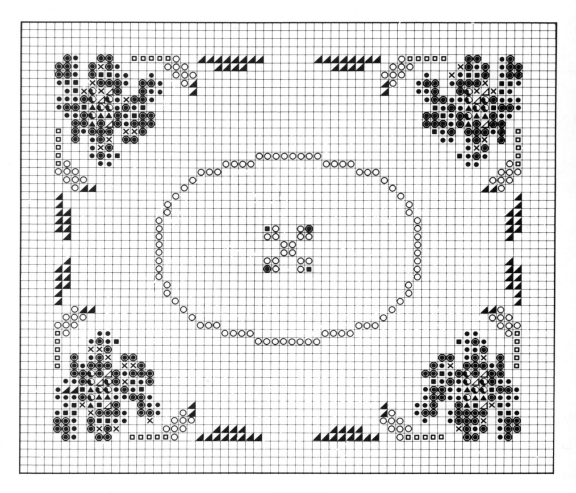

PILLOW

☐ Ecru 4000

◣ Green Wisp 79

◎ Deep Spruce 112

▣ Dark Green 22

■ Cardinal 81

● Beauty Rose 78

◉ Lt. Geranium 204

☒ Dark Pink 174

◿ Night Shadow 52

▲ Navy Blue 49

◖ Chestnut 265

Shamrock Afghan

SIZE: Finished size approximately 48 inches by 58 inches.

MATERIALS: worsted-weight yarn: 10 skeins (215-yard skeins); crochet hook size F or size required to achieve recommended gauge.

GAUGE: Crochet square = 9 inches after blocking

Be sure to check your gauge before starting. Use any size hook that will give the correct stitch gauge. If your gauge is not correct or if you make adjustments in the size of the afghan, the yarn amounts may not be sufficient.

Note: Work all rounds from right side.

SQUARE: (make 30) Ch 16, join with sl st in first st of ch to form lp, * ch 15, join with sl st in same st as previous sl st; repeat from * twice more—4 lps. Fasten off.
Rnd 2: With lp on hook, sl st in any ch-15 lp, ch 3, work 11 dc in same lp— 12 dc counting beg ch-3 as 1 dc. * 12 dc in next lp, repeat from * twice more, join with sl st in first dc—48 dc. Do not turn, continue around.
Rnd 3: (picot lp rnd) Work 1 sc in next (2nd) dc of 12-dc group, * make a picot lp as follows: ch 5, sl st in 3rd ch from hook to form picot, ch 2 to complete picot lp, sk next 2 dc, 1 sc in next dc *. Repeat between *'s twice more, make picot lp, ** sk last dc of group and first dc of next group, 1 sc in next dc. Repeat between *'s 3 times, make picot lp, repeat from ** twice more, end by skipping last dc of last group, join with sl st in first sc—16 picot lps.
Rnd 4: Work 1 sc in ch-2 sp to right of first picot, * ch 7, sc in ch-2 sp to right of next picot. Repeat from * 14 times more, ch 7, join with sl st in first sc— 16 ch-7 lps.
Rnd 5: (picot lp rnd) Work 1 sl st in each st to center of first ch-7 lp, work 1 sc in same lp, make picot lp, ** work 1 sc, ch 15 and 1 sc all in next ch-7 lp for corner, make picot lp, * 1 sc in next lp, make picot lp *. Repeat between *'s twice more; repeat from ** twice more, work 1 sc, ch 15, 1 sc all in next lp, make picot lp. Repeat between *'s twice, join with sl st in first sc—4 corner lps and 4 picot lps on each side.
Rnd 6: 1 sc in ch-2 sp to right of first picot, ch 6, ** 12 dc in corner lp, ch 6, * 1 sc in ch-2 sp to right of next picot, ch 6 *. Repeat between *'s 3 times more, repeat from ** twice, 12 dc in next corner lp, ch 6. Repeat between *'s 3 times, join with sl st in first sc.
Rnd 7: (picot lp rnd) Sl st in each st to center of first ch-6 lp, 1 sc in same lp, ** make picot lp, sk 1 dc, 1 sc in next dc, * make picot lp, sk 2 dc, 1 sc in next dc *. Repeat between *'s once and mark last picot for corner. Repeat between *'s once more, make picot lp, sk last dc, 1 sc in next ch-6 lp, (make picot lp, 1 sc in next ch-6 lp) 4 times. Repeat from ** 3 times, omitting last sc on last repeat. Join last picot lp with sl st in first sc—36 picot lps. Fasten off.

Blocking: With wrong side up and using rustproof pins, pin each square on pressing board to measure 9 inches square. Steam lightly with moderately hot iron over a wet cloth, taking care not to let weight of iron rest upon any one spot. Allow to dry before removing from board.

To Join Squares: With right side of a square facing, join yarn with sl st in first picot to left of any marked corner picot, ch 3. With wrong side of a 2nd square facing, insert hook *from wrong to right side* in first picot to left of any marked corner picot. Work sl st, ch 3; from right side, work sl st in next picot on first square, * ch 3. From wrong side, work sl st in next picot on 2nd square, ch 3. From right side, work sl st in next picot on first square. Repeat from * 6 times more, end at next corner picot on first square. Fasten off.

Continue to join squares in this way, having 5 squares in width and 6 squares in length. Work small motif to fill in space at inner corner of every 4 squares as follows: From right side, join yarn in any marked picot, ch 3, yo hook twice, insert hook in next marked picot and draw up a lp (4 lps on hook), * yo and draw through 2 lps, yo and draw through 2 lps * (2 lps on hook); yo hook twice, draw up a lp in next marked picot (5 lps on hook); repeat between *'s (3 lps on hook); yo hook twice, draw up a lp in next marked picot (6 lps on hook); repeat between *'s; yo and draw through remaining 4 lps. Fasten securely. Fill in all spaces. Steam lightly.

Outstanding Knit Irish Lace

Shown on page 48

SIZE: approximately 46½ × 64 inches including fringe.

MATERIALS: worsted-weight yarn (215 yards per skein); 10 skeins. Knitting needles size 10 or size required to achieve recommended gauge. Cable needle. Size I crochet hook (for fringe).

GAUGE: 12 sts = 3 inches
5 rows = 1 inch

Be sure to check your gauge before starting. Use any size needles that will give the correct stitch gauge. If your gauge is not correct or if you make adjustments in the size of the afghan, the yarn amounts may not be sufficient.

Special Note: On all cable strips between openwork strips, the cable twist is worked on the *7th row,* then on every *8th row.* On all *other* cable strips, the cable twist is worked on the *7th row,* then on every *16th and 8th row,* alternating. Keep careful count of the rows worked.

Afghan consists of 3 panels, each worked separately, then sewn together.

Note: Slip stitches as to purl, *except* when decreasing. Then slip as to knit.

RIGHT PANEL: Cast on 60 sts.

Pattern:
Row 1: (right side) K1, p1, k6, p1, k6, * yo, sl 1, k1, psso, k1, k2tog, yo, k6; repeat from * 3 times more, p1.
Rows 2, 4 and 6: P all sts.
Row 3: K1, p1, k6, p1, k6, *k1, yo, sl 1, k2tog, psso the k2tog, yo, k1, k6; repeat from * 3 times more, p1.
Row 5: Repeat Row 1.
Row 7: CABLE TWIST ROW: K1, p1, sl next 3 sts to cn and hold at *back* of work; k next 3 sts, k3 sts from cn

(cable twist made), p1; work cable twist on next 6 sts as before; * k1, yo, sl 1, k2tog, psso the k2tog, yo, k1; work cable twist on next 6 sts; repeat from * 3 times more, p1.
Row 8: P all sts.
Rows 9–14: Repeat Rows 1–6.
Row 15: CABLE TWIST ROW: K1, p1, k6, p1, k6, * k1, yo, sl 1, k2tog, psso the k2tog, yo, k1; work cable twist on next 6 sts; repeat from * twice more, k1, yo, sl 1, k2tog, psso the k2tog, yo, k1, k6, p1.
Row 16: P all sts.
Rows 17–23: Repeat Rows 1–7.
Row 24: P all sts.
Repeat Rows 1–24 10 times more. Repeat Rows 1–3 once more. End on right side—267 rows total. Bind off as to p.

LEFT PANEL: Cast on 60 sts.

Pattern:
Row 1: (right side) P1, k6, * yo, sl 1, k1, psso, k1, k2tog, yo, k6; repeat from * 3 times more; p1, k6, p1, k1.
Rows 2, 4 and 6: P all sts.
Row 3: P1, k6, * k1, yo, sl 1, k2tog, psso the k2tog, yo, k1, k6; repeat from * 3 times more; p1, k6, p1, k1.
Row 5: Repeat Row 1.
Row 7: CABLE TWIST ROW: P1, work cable twist on next 6 sts, * k1, yo, sl 1, k2tog, psso the k2tog, yo, k1; work cable twist on next 6 sts; repeat from * 3 times more, p1; cable twist on next 6 sts, p1, k1.
Row 8: P all sts.
Rows 9–14: Repeat Rows 1–6.
Row 15: CABLE TWIST ROW: P1, k6, * k1, yo, sl 1, k2tog, psso the k2tog, yo, k1; work cable twist on next 6 sts; repeat from * twice more, k1, yo, sl 1, k2tog, psso the k2tog, yo, k1, k6, p1, k6, p1, k1.
Row 16: P all sts.
Rows 17–23: Repeat Rows 1–7.
Row 24: P all sts.
Repeat Rows 1–24 10 times more. Repeat Rows 1–3 one time more; end

on right side—267 rows total. Bind off as to p.

CENTER PANEL: Cast on 63 sts.

Pattern:

Row 1: (right side) P1, k6, * yo, sl 1, k1, psso, k1, k2tog, yo, k6; repeat from * 4 times more, p1.

Rows 2, 4 and 6: P all sts.

Row 3: P1, k6, * k1, yo, sl 1, k2tog, psso the k2tog, yo, k1, k6; repeat from * 4 times more, p1.

Row 5: Repeat Row 1.

Row 7: CABLE TWIST ROW: P1, work cable twist on next 6 sts, * k1, yo, sl 1, k2tog, psso the k2tog, yo, k1; work cable twist on next 6 sts; repeat from * 4 times more, p1.

Row 8: P all sts.

Rows 9–14: Repeat Rows 1–6.

Row 15: CABLE TWIST ROW: P1, k6, * k1, yo, sl 1, k2tog, psso the k2tog, yo, k1; work cable twist on next 6 sts; repeat from * 3 times more, k1, yo, sl 1, k2tog, psso the k2tog, yo, k1, k6, p1.

Row 16: P all sts.

Rows 17–23: Repeat Rows 1–7.

Row 24: P all sts.

Repeat Rows 1–24 10 times more. Repeat Rows 1–3 one time more; end on right side—267 rows total. Bind off as to p.

FINISHING: With wrong side facing, pin each panel to approximately 15½ × 56 inches. Steam lightly. With cast-on edges at lower edge, matching rows and taking care to keep seams as elastic as knitted fabric, from right side sew left edge of right panel to right edge of center panel, right edge of left panel to left edge of center panel. Steam seams lightly.

Fringe: Wind fringe around 4½-inch piece of cardboard. Cut at one end. Knot a 2-strand fringe in first cast-on and every 2nd st across. Fringe bound-off edge same way.